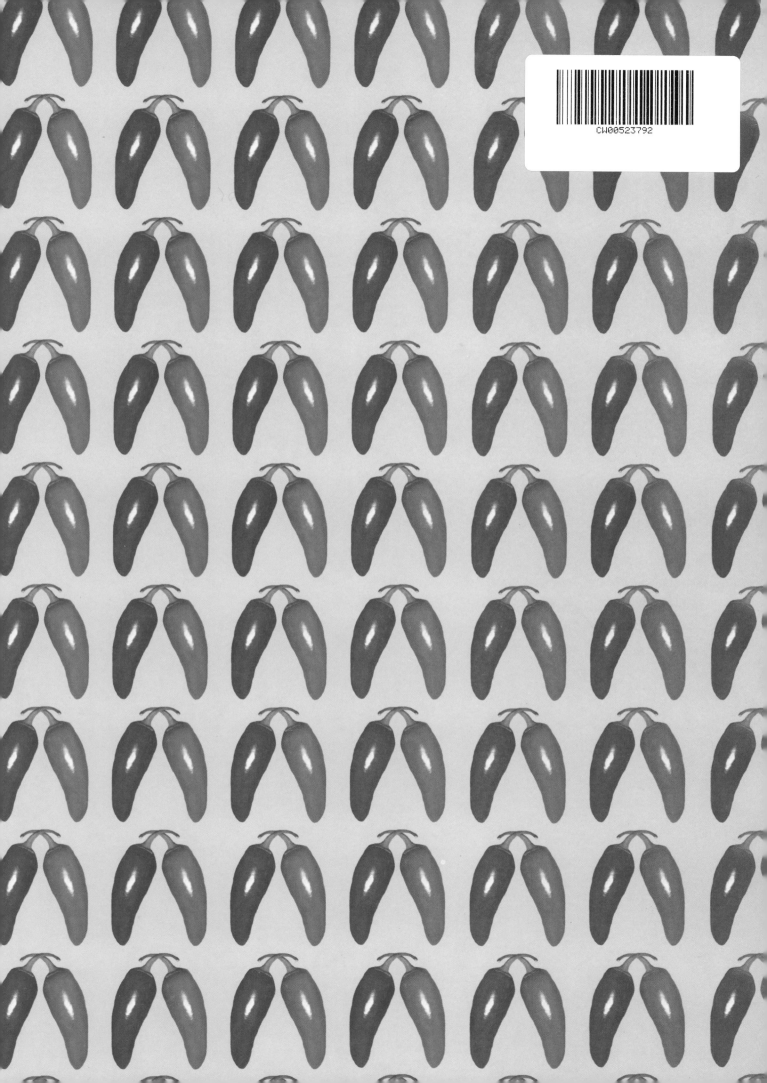

First published 1998

© Copyright Text by Caroline Knight. 1998

ISBNs :   0-9526051-1-2

C. K. Publisher,
33 The Stour,
Grange Estate,
Daventry,
Northamptonshire,
NN11 4PR.
England

Food Preparation by : Caroline Knight
Typeset by : Wah Kiew Printing Co. Sdn. Bhd.
Art and Design by : Wah Kiew Printing Co. Sdn. Bhd.
Edited by : Jess Oakes
Photography by : Mike Silver

Printed and bound in Malaysia by
Wah Kiew Printing Co. Sdn. Bhd.
No. 8249, Jalan 222,
46100 Petaling Jaya,
Selangor Darul Ehsan,
Malaysia.

FEAST FROM THE EAST

Dedication

I dedicate this book
To
My son Marco and Lisa Grove
My daughter Donna and Edwin Baris
Mr brother Mr Chuah Teik Sun
My aunt Mrs Khang Hang Poh

With all my love

By Caroline Knight

Market Scenery

Fish Stall

Fruit Stall

Barbeque Chicken

CONTENTS

ACKNOWLEDGEMENT

I would like to thank the following people for their help in preparing this book:
They are :

My favourite aunt Mrs Khang Hang Poh, who has donated many of her recipes.	PENANG
My brother Chuah Teik Sun, Mrs Tang Pai Choo	PENANG
My friend Mariko Negi for her generous recipes	JAPAN
Miss Jasmin Soo, Lai Ngoh	KUALA LUMPUR
Mrs Lubnar Unis	PAKISTAN
Mrs Amy Lim	PHILIPPINE
Mrs Tang Choo Moi	SINGAPORE
Mrs Lee Su Chen	TAIWAN

I would also like to thank Mr Takashi Ohashi for designing the Japanese Kanji Style calligraphy on the front cover of my book.

Thanks to Andrew Kendall for doing the inside cover of my book
(Picture of chillies background).

Thanks to Jess Oakes for her editorial help.

Many thanks to all my friends who helped me cook and display the food.

Cheryl Reynolds, Kerry Rowbotham, Emma Knight, Vicky Haynes, my son Marco Grove and David Cole.

And thanks to : Maggie Carthew, Pam Fox, Kathy Healey, Janet Hutchinson, Donna Bray, Elaine Balshaw, Rebecca Mabey, Hannah Clarke, Geoff Clark for their assistance.

"I like to wish you all happy cooking."

Caroline Knight

FEAST FROM THE EAST
BY
CAROLINE KNIGHT

INTRODUCTION

I have written this book especially for those people who love eating Eastern food. I have made the recipes very easy to follow. Most of the ingredients should be available from any local supermarket.

PENANG (MALAYA)

I was born on Penang Island off the coast of Malaya. At the tender age of 9 my mother started to teach me how to cook. First she showed me how to cook rice and noodles which is the staple diet of most Malaysian meals. A favourite of mine was "Malayan Chicken Curry" cooked with coconut milk. Other dishes I enjoyed were "Spareribs in Soya Sauce" and "Laksa" Spicy Noodle Soup. When I visit home to stay with my aunt, I always ask her to prepare these meals for me.

When I married and came to live in England, I realised how much I missed the mouth-watering dishes of Malaya. I have decided to write this book to share my knowledge with you all. I hope you will enjoy eating and cooking the recipes that I have chosen.

The three main nationalities in Malaya are Malay, Chinese and Indian. The most popular Malayan favourites are "Malayan Satay with Peanut Sauce", "Chicken Soup" ,"Gulai Ayam", and "Devil Chicken curry". The most popular Chinese food is "Char Koay Teow", Stir Fried Noodles, "Hokkien Mee" and "Laksa" and of course "Chinese Chicken Curry" cooked with coconut milk. A favourite Indian dish is "Murtabak" which is a pancake filled with meat and vegetables. Other dishes are "Nasi Kandar", "Daging Lembu" curry with biryani rice, and "Roti Chenan" with Dahl sauce, another type of pancake.

Malacca is south of Kuala Lumpur. Because of the Intermarriage between the Straits Chinese girls and Malay men from Penang and Singapore the women are called "Nonyas" and the men are called "Babas". The women like to perfume their food and to cook with coconut milk, which tastes really nice. This type of food is very popular in Malacca, it is called "Nonya- food". Other dishes served are "Nasi Lemak", "Fish cooked in tamarind sauce" and "Beef cooked with Tofu" which are served in many local restaurants.

SINGAPORE

From Malacca I took a train down south to the island of Singapore. It is quite cheap to eat out in restaurants. "Singapore chilli crabs" are very popular, which are delicious and spicy. Other dishes are "Singapore Fried rice" and "Egg Noodle Soup" which I like. Chinatown is another good place to eat.

TOKYO (JAPAN)

When I was a little girl I dreamt of going to Japan one day and dressing in a beautiful silk kimono. Eventually my dream came true. I arrived in the "The Land Of The Rising Sun". On my first journey to Japan I visited the small town of Koiwa which is on the outskirts of Tokyo. I stayed at a traditional Japanese Inn. For my breakfast I enjoyed fried fish, pickled vegetables, seaweed served with rice, followed by a beverage of green tea (a type of herbal tea different from British tea). After shopping around in Tokyo, I took the bullet train (the "Shinkansen") down south to the small town of Gifu. Food was sold on the train. I bought the "Bento" which is a lacquered box packed with sushis and a variety of meat and vegetables. I found it quite tasty. I really enjoyed eating it. I arrived at my friend's house and she cooked especially for me the famous "Sukiyaki" which is really delicious. She showed me how she makes "Sushi Rolls, Tempura, Sushi Rice with vegetables and soup dishes ". I was served with a cup of green tea which is supposed to be good for your health. Sushi is also very good for your diet too. I missed the food very much but I have brought back many recipes to put in this book for you to try. My next stop was Kyoto, a big city 90 miles south of Gifu. When I was in Kyoto I ate a lot of noodle soup and sushi rice with vegetables.

Then I went to Osaka which is another bustling town. I tried the food in one of the side restaurants and I ate "Stewed Tofu with seaweed, carrots and Connyaku" (which looks something like Jelly pieces). Then I made my way back up north to Chinatown in Yokohama. Chinatown is a big area which has lots of restaurants and shops selling everything from gifts, silks to foods, especially on Central Street. You must try the food there - it is so delicious!

My next stop was at Idibashi which is another town on the outskirts of Tokyo. I tried the restaurant opposite my hotel. I had porridge with chicken, mushrooms and vegetables. It is very tasty. I really enjoyed eating it.

BALI (INDONESIA)

My next destination was Denpasar, Bali. The next morning, for breakfast I had tomato and egg omelette with toast, a bowl of fresh tropical fruits and sugar cane tea or coffee. For dinner I had "Babi Pangang" which is barbecued pork with rice, and "Mee Goreng" that is Stir fried noodles. It was sumptious, I really enjoyed it. My next stop was a town called "Ubud" which has a big forest with lots of monkeys. I went to a restaurant with friends and ordered "Tereyaki Steaks" with chips, sauce and salad vegetables. The steak was very soft and tender and tasted very nice and the sauce very tasty. I ordered a drink called "Pinacolada" and the waiter brought a big coconut with the top chopped off with straws and flowers. I also enjoyed the papaya and pineapple drinks and the banana pancake.

BANGKOK (THAILAND)

My next destination was Bangkok the capital of Thailand. For lunch we went to a restaurant and I ordered a meal called "Steamboat" which is a steamer filled with soup, placed on the middle of the table on a charcoal stove. There were many plates of fresh fish, meat, prawns, mushrooms and vegetables. When the soup is boiled, meat and vegetables are dropped into the soup for 2 to 3 minutes, then brought out to serve with rice, sauce and soup. It was very tasty indeed. Chinese tea was served on the table. Next morning I was taken to The Rose Garden where elephants do many tricks and disco dancing. We had lunch at a nice cosy restaurant and I ordered

"Tom-Yam" a Spicy Prawn Soup served with rice. This is very appetizing, hot and spicy and I loved the king prawns. They are my favourite along with "Sweet and Sour Pork". Another dish is the "Pandan Chicken" which is chicken thigh wrapped in Pandan leaf grilled on open charcoal fire. It's delicious!

KOWLOON (HONG KONG)

My next stop was Kowloon the capital of Hong Kong. After touring around the island of Hong Kong and a visit to the Sung Dynasty Village where an ancient Chinese Wedding ceremony took place, the bride being carried on a Sedan Chair to the groom's house. Then I went to have lunch at the "Floating Restaurant". I had water melon soup for starter followed by "Sweet Sour Pork with rice and stir fried vegetables." Chinese tea (Jasmin Tea) is very popular in Hong Kong. For breakfast I had "Dim-Sum", which is a steamed dumpling filled with pork or chicken.

MANILA (PHILIPPINES)

My next destination was Manila the capital of the Philippines. The main crops are rubber, coffee, pineapples, bananas, maize, sugar cane and coconuts. The most important rice- producing area is the lowland area of Luzon. The most impressive man-made sight is the spectacular series of irrigated rice terraces that contour the mountain slopes in the northern interior. These were constructed by Igoro tribesmen, who are descendants of some of the first people to colonize the Philippines.

The island of Cebu is about 45 minutes southeast of Luzon Island by air. Mainly maize is grown here, which is the staple food of the local diet. Food here is reasonably cheap. Barbecued fish or chicken on a spit costs about 35 pesos (about 60p). Food like pork (Godobo) is very popular, as is chicken curry and sweet and sour pork. Coke costs about 10 pesos (10p) a bottle. The people here eat a lot of fish.

LAHORE (PAKISTAN)

The capital of Pakistan was IslamaBad. Lahore is a big bustling town in the Punjab District. The main breakfast is "Chappati" which is a pancake fried in butter also known as "Parapta" with fried egg. For lunch people normally have a light snack like "Pakoras" or "Samosas" with 1 or 2 pitta bread. For dinner people normally have lamb or chicken curry with chappati or rice, salad (cucumber, tomato and onion slices) and yoghurt. Their favourite food are kebabs, pulau rice, chappati with lamb curry dishes. People like to eat hot curries with plenty of spices, using red dried chillies, green chillies and chat masala and salt for their cooking.

TAIWAN (FORMOSA)

Taiwan is a small island about 400 kilo metre long and 36,000 kilo metre wide situated on the east of China. Population is 21,000. Things are much cheaper to buy in Taiwan. Food are quite reasonable to eat at restaurants like Stir Fried Rice, Steamed Meat Dumplings, Chicken Rice, Braised Pork in brown sauce. Soup is served at every meal. Clamp with ginger soup, Won Ton, Tomato and onion with beef soup. For breakfast people eat fried vegetable cake, rice soup and drink hot soya bean milk. Other dishes are Roast duck, Chicken Noodles and Stir Fried Mixed Vegetables. Rice is mainly grown on the lowlands of Taipei.

BEEF ROLL
(JAPANESE STYLE)

Cooking time: 15 minutes
Preparation time: 7 minutes

5 oz (150 g) beef slice (1 inch wide)
1/3 burdock (long brown thin vegetable)
10 leaves beef steak plants (known as perillas)
1/3 teaspoon sugar
1 tablespoon soya sauce
1 tablespoon olive oil
A pinch of Aji-no-moto (Gourmet Powder)
A pinch of salt
A pinch of pepper

METHOD:

1. Peel the burdock and cut into 1/4 inch wide and 2 inches long. Soak in water for 15 to 20 minutes to remove harshness.

2. Boil the burdock about 5 minutes and leave on one side.

3. Spread the sliced meat and divide it into 10. Add salt and pepper to the meat on both sides.

4. Spread the sliced meat onto a perilla leaf or cabbage leaf, then put 1 burdock stick on the leaf and roll.

5. Heat the pan and oil it. Fry the rolled meat with sugar, soya sauce and a pinch of Aji-nomoto. Serve with Shimeji sotay or carrot sotay.

TIPS:

If perilla leaf is not available, use cabbage leaf for substitute.

MALAYAN BEEF CURRY

Cooking time : 1 hour
Preparation time : 20 minutes

1.2 lb (500 g) topside beef (cut into small cubes)
1/2 cup thick coconut milk
2 cups thin coconut milk
2 tablespoons vegetable oil
Salt to taste
12 shallots (peeled and finely sliced)
4 cloves garlic (peeled and finely sliced)
3 slices ginger (peeled and finely shredded)

INGREDIENTS TO BE BLENDED:

10 dried chillies (half seeded) soak in water until soft. Drain away rest of the water.
4 red fresh chillies (seeded)
2 dessertspoons Jintan Puteh (small dark cummin seeds)
1 piece yellow ginger (3 cm) or 1 teaspoon turmeric
2 stalks lemon grass (use 6 inch from the root upwards) crushed. Discard top.

METHOD:

1. Boil 2 cups of thin coconut milk in a medium saucepan. Reduce heat a little and add the beef, shallots, garlic, ginger and salt. Stir for 1 minute and cover pan with lid and simmer until beef is tender about 30 to 40 minutes.

2. Once the meat is tender push meat to one side and add the blended paste and stir into the oil for 2 minutes on medium heat until medium brown.

3. Then mix the meat with the thick coconut milk and salt. Taste to see if you need more salt. Simmer until the curry reduces itself and becomes dry and the oil shows up. Serve with boiled rice.

TIPS:

Lemon grass is also known as "serai " in Malay language. If lemon grass is not available, use 2 tablespoons of lemon juice for a substitute.
Small dark cummin seed is known as "Jintan Puteh"

KIMPAP
(KOREAN BEEF DISH)

Cooking time: 25 minutes
Preparation time: 10 minutes

Serves 4

2 cups rice
2¼ cups water
½ lb (225 g) lean beef (cut into thin strips)
2 tablespoons soya sauce
1 spring onion (finely chopped)
1 tablespoon sesame oil
1 yellow pickled radish (cut into thin strips)
1 raw carrot (cut into thin strips)
4 eggs separated (fry and cut into thin strips)
½ cup cooked spinach
1 tablespoon pepper threads (cut into fine strips)
20 full sized sheets laver (seaweed)

METHOD:

1. Wash and cook rice with 2¼ cups of water until soft and fluffy. It should take 25 minutes to cook the rice. Switch off and then let it settle for 10 minutes before serving.

2. Cut beef into thin strips. Heat wok with oil. When hot add beef and fry with soya sauce for 15 to 20 minutes until beef is cooked.

3. Beat the eggs in a bowl. Heat a small frying pan with 1 tablespoon of oil until quite hot. Pour the eggs to cover the pan thinly cook until light brown and then turn over for 1 minute.

4. Repeat four more times until it is used up. When cool cut into fine strips.

5. Boil the spinach for 2 to 3 minutes. Cut the carrots, radish, red pepper into thin strips.

6. First lay a sheet of laver (seaweed) on the board. Cover with a thin layer of rice.

7. Lay strips of beef, radish, carrot, egg, spinach and pepper threads.

8. Roll it up like a jelly (like sushi roll). A bamboo roller helps.

9. Use a sharp knife cut the roll into ¾ inch slices.

Serve on a plate and dip in chilli or tomato sauce.

TIPS:

KIMPAP is a very popular snack or lunch food, it's a roll something like Japanese Sushi but does not use raw fish.

KOREAN FOOD is always served with Kimchi and at least 3 to 4 side dishes. These vary with the season and are often the most delicious part of the meal. There are hundreds of variaties of Kimchi.

Kimchi is a cabbage or radish preserved with chilli pepper. It can be stored for months. It used to be their source of vegetable during the cold winter months. It is still the most important food for Koreans.

Koreans use Kimchi to cook many of their recipes. You can buy Kimchi from Chinese and Japanese Supermarkets.

BULGOGI (KOREAN DISH)
BEEF (LETTUCE WRAP)

Cooking time: 25 minutes
Preparation time: 10 minutes

Serves 4

1 lb beef (450 g)
2 tablespoons soya sauce
1 tablespoon sugar
1 tablespoon sesame oil
1/2 teaspoon salt
1/8 teaspoon black pepper
4 medium spring onions (coarsely chopped)
3 to 4 cloves garlic (finely chopped)
1 teaspoon fresh ginger (finely chopped)
2 teaspoons water
2 tablespoons rice wine or white wine

METHOD:

1. Cut beef into very thin strips.

2. Marinate beef in a pyrex or dish with soya sauce, sugar, black pepper, rice wine, ginger, garlic, for about 2 hours or overnight.

3. Grill or broil on a grill or hot plate or stir-fry for about 15 minutes.

4. Bulgogi is often served as a lettuce wrap. First wash and rinse lettuce, use to wrap meat.

5. Put a piece of lettuce on a plate. The meat is put onto the lettuce with slices of raw garlic and green sliced chillies and chilli paste. Chilli paste is made from chillies, spring onions, sesame oil and garlic.

TIPS:

All Korean food is served with a bowl of rice. BULGOGI is a traditional broiled or grilled beef dish. Pork can be cooked the same way.

BEEF IN PORTUGUESE SAUCE

Cooking time: 40 minutes
Preparation time: 15 minutes

Serves 4

12 oz (350 g) fillet steak or sirloin steak
$1/2$ onion (peeled and sliced)
1 red and 1 green pepper (cut into small pieces)
2 tablespoons vegetable oil or olive oil

SEASONINGS:

2 teaspoons light soya sauce
1 tablespoon dark soya sauce
$1/2$ teaspoon salt
1 dessertspoon sugar
$1/4$ teaspoon sesame oil
A pinch of ground pepper
1 medium sized egg
2 teaspoons white wine

SAUCE:

4 tablespoons coconut milk
4 tablespoons evaporated milk
$1/2$ teaspoon salt
$1/2$ teaspoon sugar
2 teaspoons cornflour mixed with 2 tablespoons of water to make it creamy.

METHOD:

1. Finely slice the beef and the onions. Cut peppers into small squares.

2. Mix the seasonings in a bowl and add the beef, mix well and cover with lid and marinate for 30 minutes.

3. To prepare the sauce, put coconut milk, evaporated milk, into a small saucepan over low heat. Stir for 2 to 3 minutes add salt, sugar and then cornflour and continue stirring until sauce is creamy but not too thick. Add a little water if necessary so that the sauce is not too thick.

4. Heat the wok with 2 tablespoons of oil until quite hot, add the onions and stir until medium brown for about 2 minutes. Then add beef and stir until well mixed for about 10 minutes. Add green and red peppers and stir for 5 minutes.

5. Then add the sauce mixture and keep stirring. Simmer for 20 to 30 minutes until meat is tender. Add more water if necessary so that the sauce does not get too thick.

CHICKEN OR BEEF TERIYAKI
(INDONESIAN STYLE)

Cooking time: 35 minutes
Preparation time: 15 minutes

Serves 4

4 Chicken breasts
or 4 beef steaks
2 to 3 tablespoons Indonesian sweet soya sauce
A pinch of salt
A pinch of pepper
4 to 5 oz butter or margarine
2 to 3 tablespoons tomato sauce

SAUCE:

Melt the butter in a small saucepan for 2 minutes. Then add the sweet soya sauce, garlic, tomato sauce, black pepper and salt and stir for 2 minutes and turn off heat.

METHOD:

1. Wash the chicken breasts or beef steaks and pat dry with paper towel. Sprinkle with salt and pepper on both sides. Leave for 5 minutes before grilling.

2. Grill meat for 8 to 10 minutes on either sides until brown. Pierce with a skewer to see if meat is cooked. Transfer onto 4 plates.

3. Pour the sauce over the chicken or beef steaks and serve with rice, carrots and peas.

MASAMAN
(THAI BEEF DISH)

Cooking time: 30 minutes
Preparation time: 10 minutes

Serves 4

2 lb (907 g) beef (sirloin)
1 small tin coconut milk
or 1 packet dried coconut milk
1/2 packet Masaman chilli sauce
8 oz (200g) small potatoes
1 small packet salted peanuts
2 teaspoons sugar
2 to 3 tablespoons tamarind juice
2 tablespoons vegetable oil

METHOD:

1. Wash beef, pat dry with paper towel and cut into 1 inch cubes. Put into a pressure cooker and steam for 10 to 15 minutes until soft. Soak tamarind fruit in a cup of water for 10 minutes. Save the juice and set aside for later. Discard the stones.

2. Heat wok with oil until quite hot on medium heat, add the masaman sauce and stir fry for 1 minute until red in colour. Then reduce heat and add coconut milk and stir for 1 minute.

3. Add beef, sugar, potatoes, peanuts, tamarind juice and mix well and boil for 8 minutes and simmer for 5 minutes. Add salt to taste. Serve with rice and vegetable salad.

TIPS:
Masaman sauce is sold in packets in any Chinese or Thai Supermarkets.

NUA OB THAI DERM
(THAI ROAST BEEF)

Cooking time: 25 minutes
Preparation time: 10 minutes

Serves 4

400 g beef (cut into 1/2 inch thick strips)
6 cloves of garlic (peeled)
4 tablespoons coriander (chopped from the root end)
  (Reserve the leaves for garnish)
3 tablespoons fish soy sauce (Nam Pla)
3 tablespoons vegetable oil
1 litre beef stock (1 beef cake per litre water)
250 g (9 oz)green beans (cleaned and roughly chopped)
2 onions (peeled and chopped)

METHOD:

1. Place the garlic, chopped coriander, oil, pepper and fish sauce in a mortar and pound to a thick paste or blend to a thick paste.

2. Marinate the beef in this mixture for about an hour. After one hour scrape the marinade off the beef and set it aside for later.

3. Heat the saucepan when hot add the steaks and fry for about 8 minutes until brown on both sides. Add the remaining marinade and stock and simmer on low heat for 15 minutes until the gravy is quite thick and the meat is tender.

4. Boil the green beans with water in another saucepan for approximately 2 minutes and drain.

5. Remove the beef steaks and place them on a serving dish. Pour half of the gravy over the steaks, leaving the other half in the saucepan to continue cooking with the beans and onions. Once cooked, pour vegetables over the steaks and garnish with coriander leaves. Serve with boiled rice.

NIKUJYAGA
(BEEF AND POTATOES)

Cooking time: 25 minutes
Preparation time: 7 minutes

Serves 4

11 oz (300 g) beef (finely sliced and cut into 2 inch length)
6 small potatoes (peeled and cut into halves)
1 1/2 cups of dashi soup
3 tablespoons soya sauce
2/3 teaspoon salt
2/3 tablespoon sugar
2 tablespoons Japanese wine (Sake)
1 medium onion (finely sliced)
6 oz konnyaku or use (100 g) peas

METHOD:

1. Oil and heat the pan, add beef and stir fry for 3 minutes, then add salt and pepper.

2. Add potatoes, dashi soup, soya sauce, sugar and Sake and cook on medium heat for about 20 minutes. When the soup is boiled, serve onto a flat plate.

3. Add onions and thread konnyaku or green peas can be added to this dish.

TIPS:

This is only a side dish can be eaten with rice. Can also be eaten with soup and salad vegetables.

Connyaku is made from potatoes and comes in the form of a shredded jelly or sold in square pieces which can be cut into smaller pieces. To substitute use transparent Chinese noodles. Dashi soup is sold in dry packet, available in Japanese or Chinese supermarkets. One packet of Dashi soup can make up to 5 cups in quantity.

GYU- DON
(BEEF STIR- FRY)

Cooking time : 25 minutes
Preparation time : 5 minutes

Serves 4

250 g beef (finely sliced)
200 g thread (shape) konnyaku (potato jelly)
A bunch of spring onions (cut diagonally)
3 medium eggs
2 tablespoon vegetable or olive oil
3 cups of rice with 3 cups of water to boil

METHOD:

1. First wash and cook rice with 3 cups of water for 25 minutes until soft and fluffy.

2. Heat the frying pan with oil, when hot add beef and stir fry. Add $1^1/2$ tablespoons of sugar and one tablespoon of soya sauce.

3. Next add konnyaku and stir fry, then add spring onions and taste it. Add the blended eggs at the end of cooking and mix well together.

4. Put cooked rice into 4 individual bowls and serve with beef.

TIPS:

This is another popular dish in Japan. Gyu means beef and Don is the same as Oyako Don in the other recipe.
If konnyaku is not available, use transparent Chinese noodles for substitute.
Soak noodle in water for 5 minutes until soft and drain.

MA-BO-DO-FU (CHINESE STYLE)
(TOFU WITH BEEF IN CHILLI BEAN SAUCE)

Cooking time: 20 minutes
Preparation time: 15 minutes

Serves 4

1 carton white Tofu (square)
7 oz (200 g) minced beef
1 tablespoon sesame oil
1 onion (finely chopped)
3 cloves of garlic (chopped)
1 dessertspoon chilli bean sauce (To Ban Jyan)
A small amount of miso paste
3 to 4 spring onions (chopped)
1 dessertspoon cornflour

METHOD:

1. Heat the wok with sesame oil until quite hot, add the minced beef, onions and garlic and stir fry for about 7 minutes. Then add spring onions and stir for 2 minutes.

2. Cut the Tofu into small squares and add to the beef mixture and continue stirring for 2 to 3 minutes. Reduce heat, add To Ban Jyan chilli sauce and miso paste and stir again. Mix cornflour with a little water to a cream and add to the sauce.

3. Taste it to see if you need more chilli sauce or a little more water. Turn off heat and serve with rice.

TIPS:
Put the Tofu on a plate and press lightly to squeeze off water.

INDIAN BEEF CURRY (PENANG STYLE)
(GULAI DAGING LEMBU)

Cooking time: 40 minutes
Preparation time: 15 minutes

Serves 4

2 lb (907 g) beef or lamb
4 oz (100 g) curry powder
2 tablespoons coriander powder
2 large onions (finely sliced)
2 cinnamon sticks (kayu puteh)
(3 to 4 star anise)
2 inch (5 cm) fresh ginger (sliced)
4 to 5 cloves garlic (bawang puteh) chopped
4 fresh red chillies (sliced) or cut into half
2 tablespoons vegetable oil
1¹/₂ pints water (900 ml)
Juice of 1 lime

METHOD:

1. Wash the beef (finely sliced). Blend the ginger, garlic, 1 onion and 2 chillies into a smooth paste for 1 to 2 minutes.

2. Heat oil in a deep saucepan until quite hot, add 1 onion, star anises, cinnamon stick and fry for 2 minutes.

3. Add the meat and stir for 5 to 6 minutes. Then add curry powder and stir for 2 minutes. Add water and coconut milk and the rest of the chillies and boil for 10 to 15 minutes and simmer for 20 minutes until meat is tender.

4. During cooking add fresh chopped coriander. Add lime juice and salt to taste. Serve with boiled rice or biryani rice.

BEEF RENDANG
(MALAYSIAN STYLE)

Cooking time: 50 minutes
Preparation time: 15 minutes

Serves 4

1.5 k (3 lb) beef
3 cups coconut milk
1 cm (¹/₂") galangal (also known as lengkuas) crushed
or use 1 teaspoon "laos powder"
2 stalks lemon grass (also known as serai) crushed
A pinch of salt
2 tablespoons vegetable oil

TO MAKE PASTE:

Ingredients:

6 level tablespoons coriander (known as ketumbar)
1 tablespoon cumin (known as jintan manis)
20 to 30 dried chillies (soak in water until soft and drained)
1 cup small red onions (peeled and chopped)
2 to 3 cloves garlic
4 thin slices ginger
6 tablespoons grated roasted coconut

METHOD:

1. Prepare the beef. Cut into 1 inch cubes.

2. To make the paste, blend coriander, cumin seeds, dried chillies, red onions, garlic, ginger, and roasted coconut to a smooth paste. Add a little bit of water to the ingredients to make it easy to blend.

3. Heat a large saucepan with oil, when hot add the paste and the rest of the spices and stir-fry for 2 to 3 minutes until oil separates from the paste.

4. Next add beef and stir- fry for 2 to 3 minutes and then add coconut milk and salt. Boil meat for 10 minutes on medium heat, then reduce heat and simmer for 40 to 50 minutes until tender. (Beef takes a little bit longer to cook). Continue cooking until curry becomes dry.

TIPS:
If you prefer it mild, use half the amount of chillies or use 6 chillies.
Galangal is part of the ginger family. Soak galangal in water for about 30 to 40 minutes until soft and drained.

GRILLED CHICKEN
(UBUD STYLE BALI)

Cooking time: 40 minutes
Preparation time: 15 to 20 minutes

Serves 4

4 chicken breasts
4 potatoes (cut into finger size) deep fry
1 lb (450 g) long green beans (cut into 2 inch lengths)
1 lb (450 g) carrots (cut into 2 inch strips)
6 oz (175 g) butter or margarine
2 pints (1 litre) vegetable oil for deep frying

SAUCE INGREDIENTS:

4 tomato (sliced)
A pinch of black pepper
5 cloves of garlic (chopped)
1 medium onion (sliced)
2 tablespoons Indonesian sweet soya sauce (ketchup manis)

METHOD:

1. Wash chicken and pat dry with paper towel. Fry chicken in a pan with butter on low heat for 5 minutes each side until the chicken is white.

2. Sprinkle chicken with salt and pepper and leave for 5 minutes before grilling. Then grill chicken for 8 to 10 minutes each side until light brown. Check to see if meat is cooked.

3. Wash beans and carrots and boil them for 3 minutes until soft. Dip in batter and deep fry until light brown.

4. Deep fry the potatoes until crispy brown.

TO MAKE SAUCE:

1. Wash and slice the tomatoes and onions. Heat a small saucepan with butter until quite hot, add tomatoes and onions and stir for 3 minutes.

2. Then add sweet soya sauce and pepper and stir for 1 minute. Pour sauce into a very small bowl and put it in the centre of the plate before serving.

3. Arrange the chicken on one side of the plate, with chips, and vegetables. Serve with lettuce, cucumber, tomato and salad cream.

MALAYAN CHICKEN SATAY

This is one of my favourite dish.
It is very popular in Malaysia.

Cooking time: 25 minutes
Preparation time: 15 minutes

Makes 6 to 7 sticks

1 lb (450 g) Chicken breasts
or lamb, beef or prawns can be used
1 stalk lemon grass (finely sliced)
2 inch (cm) fresh ginger (finely sliced)
1 to 2 teaspoons aniseed powder (jintan manis)
1 to 2 teaspoons cummin powder (jintan puteh)
1 tablespoon coriander powder (ketumbah)
1 teaspoon salt
2 inch (5 cm) yellow ginger or
1 to 2 teaspoons turmeric powder
1 inch lengkuas or galangal (finely sliced)
2 tablespoons sugar
2 tablespoons vegetable oil
1/2 teaspoon red chilli powder

METHOD:

1. Heat a small saucepan with oil until quite hot then add cummin seeds, coriander, aniseed and chilli powder and stir fry until brown for 2 to 3 minutes and set aside.

2. Blend lemon grass, ginger, turmeric, and lengkuas into a smooth paste. Add a little drop of water if necessary for blending. Switch off the blender and stir with a spatula.

3. Cut chicken or meat into fine strips. Put into a pyrex with salt, sugar and the paste and mix well. Cover for 30 minutes to marinate.

4. After marinating add the rest of the spice that is cummin, coriander, aniseed and mix well and put chicken onto a metal skewer for about 6 inch length.

5. Grill for 3 to 4 minutes each side until brown, basting it with remaining marinating sauce. Turning over to the other side. Serve with cucumber slices, onion rings and boiled rice.

TIPS:
Lemon grass is also known as "serai". Use 6 inches from the root onwards.
The chicken can be marinated overnight. Use double amount of meat if you are preparing for more guests.

SATAY SAUCE
(PEANUT)

Cooking time: 15 minutes
Preparation time: 5 minutes

8 oz (225 g) roasted peanut (without skin)
1/2 onion
2 cloves of garlic
1 tablespoon brown sugar
1 tablespoon vegetable oil
1/2 teaspoon red chilli powder
1/2 cup water
1/2 teaspoon turmeric powder

METHOD:

1. First, ground the peanuts. Chop the onion and garlic.

2. Heat a small saucepan with oil on medium heat, add onions and garlic and stir fry for 2 minutes until medium brown then add water and continue stirring.

3. Add ground peanuts, sugar, chilli and turmeric powder and simmer for 10 minutes. Taste to see if you need more chilli. Now it is ready to use as a dipping sauce for Satay meat. Serve hot.

INDONESIAN ROAST CHICKEN

Cooking time: 65 minutes
Preparation time: 15 minutes

Serves 4

1.5 k (3 lb) chicken
5 cloves of garlic (chopped)
A pinch of salt
A pinch of black pepper
$1/2$ teaspoon mustard (paste)
$1/2$ teaspoon Lea and Perrins Sauce
1 tablespoon dark soya sauce
1 dessertspoon sugar
2 tablespoons of vegetable or peanut oil

METHOD:

1. Wash chicken and pat dry. Rub pepper, garlic, salt, mustard, sugar, Lea Perrins and soya sauce over the chicken. Heat a frying pan with 2 tablespoons of oil and stir fry the chicken for 10 minutes each side until slightly brown.

2. Grill the chicken over charcoal fire on a skewer, turning every 5 or 6 minutes for about 50 minutes until tender. During cooking baste the chicken with the remaining sauce using a brush.

3. Can be roasted in the oven. Wrap chicken with the seasoning in tin foil and roast for 1 hour 30 minutes until chicken is cooked. Allow 15 to 20 minutes if the chicken is larger. To test if the chicken is cooked, use a skewer to pierce the meat and that the juice is clear. The meat should be white when cooked.

Serve with fried rice, spring onions, cucumber and tomato slices.

SOUTHERN FRIED CHICKEN
(BALI STYLE)

Cooking time: 30 minutes
Preparation time: 10 minutes

Serves 4

4 Chicken legs
5 cloves garlic (chopped)
2 tablespoons vegetable oil
1 dessertspoon dark soya sauce
1 dessertspoon (chilli sauce)
2 to 3 oz margarine
4 oz double cream

METHOD:

1. Wash chicken and pat dry with paper towel. Heat the wok with oil until quite hot, add
    the chicken and stir fry for about 10 to 15 minutes. Mix the soya sauce and chilli sauce
    with the margarine and add to the chicken.

2. Turn heat down a little and add the cream and stir well, simmer for 15 minutes until
    chicken is tender. Serve with chips, salad or fried rice.

DRY FRIED MALAYAN CHICKEN

Cooking time: 30 to 35 minutes
Preparation time: 10 minutes

Serves 6 to 8

1 kilo chicken (cut into joints)
A pinch of salt
A pinch pepper
1/2 cup of water
4 tablespoons chilli powder
1 teaspoon turmeric powder
20 shallots (finely sliced)
2 sprigs curry leaves
1 onion (finely sliced)
1 tablespoon thick soya sauce
1 teaspoon jintan manis (fennel seeds)
6 tablespoons oil
1 kaffir lime

METHOD:

1. Cut the chicken into joints. Heat oil in wok until quite hot add the shallots, fennel seeds, curry leaves and chicken and stir fry for 15 minutes on medium heat.

2. Then add salt, pepper chilli, turmeric powder and continue stirring until well mixed.

3. Add water and stir the chicken until it becomes dry then add onions, soya sauce and lime juice and simmer for 15 to 20 minutes until chicken is tender. This is a very spicy dish. Serve with boiled rice.

TIPS:

The chilli powder can be quite hot. If you like it mild, reduce it by half.

CHINESE CHICKEN CURRY
(PENANG STYLE)

Cooking time: 30 minutes
Preparation time: 15 minutes

Serves 4

4 chicken breasts or thighs
2 tablespoons curry powder
1 whole medium onion or
12 small shallots (peeled and sliced)
2 cloves garlic (peeled and sliced)
2 sticks lemon grass (chopped)
1 cinnamon stick
1/2 teaspoon chilli powder
1/2 teaspoon turmeric powder
1/2 cup semi-skimmed milk
A pinch of salt
5 whole peppers
1/2 cup of water
A pinch of Aji-no-moto
2 tablespoons vegetable oil
1 dessertspoon sugar
6 to 8 small potatoes

METHOD:

1. Wash chicken and slice into half inch slices. Peel and washed potatoes.

2. Peel and slice onions and garlic. Use lemon grass 6 inches from the root upwards and slice finely. Blend the shallots, garlics and lemon grass together until the paste is smooth.

3. Mix curry powder with 1 tablespoon of water until creamy.

4. Heat a large size saucepan with 2 tablespoons of oil when hot add the paste and stir fry for 2 minutes. Then add curry powder and stir again and reduce heat.

5. Add cinnamon stick, pepper, chilli and turmeric powder and stir again for 1 minute. Next add chicken and stir fry for 10 minutes until well mixed, add milk and water and cook for 30 minutes until chicken is tender.

6. Add potatoes, salt, Aji-no-moto and sugar to taste. Prick potatoes to see if soft. Serve with boiled rice. If you like it hot, add more chilli powder.

CHICKEN RICE (INDIAN STYLE)
(PILAU RICE)

Cooking time: 45 minutes
Preparation time: 15 minutes

Serves 4

2 cups rice
5 cups water for soup
1 to 1½ lb chicken (450 g to 675 g)
3 medium onions (chopped)
5 to 6 cloves garlic (chopped)
2 teaspoons salt
2 teaspoons whole coriander
2 teaspoons fennel seeds
4½ oz (125 g) butter

SPICES:

8 to 10 whole black peppers
½ teaspoon cummin seeds
2 or 3 cinnamon sticks
4 or 5 cloves of garlic (chopped)

METHOD:

1. Wash and soak rice for about 20 to 30 minutes in saucepan.

2. Cut chicken into bite size pieces. Then prepare the soup. Put water, chicken, garlic, one onion, salt, coriander, fennel and half of the spices in a medium saucepan and boil.

3. Reduce heat to medium and simmer for about 15 minutes. Then remove the chicken from the saucepan onto a plate and sieve the soup, which will be reduced to 3 cups.

4. In another saucepan melt the butter, add chopped onions and keep stirring until golden brown. Add the chicken and the rest of the spices and stir fry for about 5 minutes.

5. Then add half a glass of water and cover the saucepan for 5 minutes. Stir and add the prepared 3 cups of soup and bring to the boil.

6. Now it is ready to add the soaked rice and cook for about 20 to 25 minutes until soft and fluffy.

Prepare the salad vegetables. Wash lettuce, half a cucumber, tomatoes, and spring onions and drain them. Finely slice the cucumber and tomatoes. Cut spring onions into 2 inch lengths. Finely slice 2 green chillies. Put all the vegetables into a large bowl and pour the vinegar sauce over the vegetables and serve.

CHICKEN MALAYSIA

Cooking time: 25 minutes
Preparation time: 15 minutes

Serves 4

1 kilo (2 lb) Chicken (cut into joints)
1 tablespoon Worcestershire sauce
10 small shallots (peeled and sliced)
4 cloves garlic (finely sliced)
1 cm fresh ginger (finely sliced)
1 stalk lemon grass (finely sliced)
use 6 inch from the root part upwards
2 teaspoons dark soya sauce
3 teaspoons sugar
A pinch of salt
2 tablespoons vegetable oil

METHOD:

1. Blend together the onion, garlic, ginger and lemon grass. Marinate the chicken with the blended ingredients.

2. Add the Worcestershire sauce, soya sauce, sugar and salt to taste.

3. Put the chicken in a pyrex dish and cover with a lid and set aside for about 2 hours.

4. Then drain the chicken pieces and add 2 tablespoons oil to the marinated sauce which will be used for basting.

5. Grill the chicken pieces on both sides until cooked, about 10 minutes each side.

6. During grilling, baste the chicken with the marinated sauce. Serve hot with salad.

AYAM KELANTAN
(GRILLED MALAYAN CHICKEN)

Cooking time: 30 minutes
Preparing time: 10 minutes

Serves 6 to 8

1 medium sized chicken
A pinch of salt
1 chicken stock cube
2 metric cups thick coconut milk
6 liman perut leaves or (2 lime leaves)
4 dried tamarind slices
2 stalks of bruised lemon grass

BLENDED INGREDIENTS:

2 cm piece fresh turmeric root (yellow ginger) or 2 teaspoons turmeric
1 tablespoon roasted coriander
2 thin slices galangal (also known as Lengkuas or Laos)
20 chilli padis (very small green chillies)
1 cm piece root ginger
4 cloves of garlic
20 small shallots or 10 big ones

METHOD:

1. Wash the chicken and cut into halves or into 4 pieces. Put all the ingredients and spices including the coconut milk with the chicken pieces in a clay pot or in a large saucepan. Bring to the boil, stirring for about 10 minutes.

2. Then remove chicken from pot and drain. Then put chicken under the grill until golden brown, basting with oil during grilling. Save the gravy which is left in the pot for later.

3. Transfer chicken pieces onto a dish. Heat the gravy sauce and pour over the chicken. Garnish with golden fried shallots, tomato slices, cucumber slices or even lettuce leaves.

CHICKEN WITH MUSHROOMS
(CHINESE STYLE)

Cooking time : 15 to 20 minutes
Preparation time: 10 minutes

2 chicken breasts (sliced into 1/2" wide pieces)
6 to 8 Chinese mushrooms (soaked in water
until soft and drained, finely sliced)
1 clove garlic (crushed)
1 large onion (finely sliced)
2 to 3 finely sliced ginger
2 dessertspoons vegetable oil
A pinch of salt
A pinch of pepper
1 dessertspoon cornflour
1/2 cup water

METHOD:

1. Wash chicken breasts, pat dry with kitchen paper. Slice into 1/2 inch wide pieces.

2. Heat wok with oil until quite hot, add garlic and onion and stir fry for 1 minute until medium brown and soft.

3. Add the chicken , salt, pepper and 1/2 cup of water and stir well. Simmer for 15 minutes, until chicken is tender, then add mushrooms and ginger and continue cooking for a further 5 minutes. Add the cornflour mix with a little water to make it creamy. Continue stirring for 1 minute.

4. Taste to see if you need more salt.

TIPS:
The mushroom water can be use for stock as it is very tasty.

CHICKEN WITH POTATOES
(PENANG STYLE)

Cooking time: 35 to 40 minutes
Preparation time: 15 minutes

Serves 4

1.5 kilo (2 lb) chicken
3 medium potatoes
1 teaspoon vegetable oil
1 medium onion (finely sliced)
1 cup diced tomatoes
1 tablespoon white wine
$1/4$ teaspoon salt
2 to 3 cloves garlic (chopped)

METHOD:

1. Wash and cut chicken into bite size pieces and rub salt all over. Peel and cut potatoes into 1 inch cubes.

2. Heat wok until quite hot, add chicken pieces and stir fry until medium brown. Sprinkle chopped garlic over the chicken, add salt and stir-fry for 15 minutes.

3. Add wine, potatoes and tomatoes and continue stirring for 5 minutes.

4. Transfer chicken and potatoes into an oven proof dish and cover with lid and bake on Gas Mark 4 350° F / 180° C for 30 minutes until chicken is tender.

LEMON CHICKEN

Cooking time: 20 minutes
Preparation time: 15 minutes

Serves 4

4 chicken breasts
Juice of 2 lemons
1 medium carrot (peeled and sliced diagonally)
2 spring onions (cut into 2 inch lengths)
1 dessertspoon sugar
1 medium onion (finely sliced)
1 cup water
1 piece fresh ginger (2.5 cm) peeled and finely sliced
A pinch of salt
1 teaspoon light soya sauce
2 to 3 tablespoons vegetable or peanut oil

METHOD:

1. Wash chicken pat dry with paper towel, slice chicken into half inch wide pieces. Wash spring onions and cut into 2 inch lengths. Wash carrots and slice diagonally and then layer them on top of one another and finely slice them again..

2. Squeeze lemon juice and put through strainer and set aside. Mix cornflour with 2 tablespoons water into a creamy mixture to thicken the sauce.

3. Heat the wok with oil until quite hot, add the onions and stir fry for 2 minutes until light brown. Add ginger and stir for 1 minute, then add the chicken and stir for 8 to 10 minutes. Then add the carrots and spring onions and stir for 1 minute.

4. Add lemon juice and 1 cup of water and bring to the boil for 5 minutes. Reduce heat add cornflour and stir. Add soya sauce, sugar, salt to taste. Simmer for 15 minutes until chicken is tender. Serve with boiled or fried rice.

SWEET AND SOUR CHICKEN
(PENANG STYLE)

Cooking time : 20 minutes
Preparation time: 15 minutes

Serves 4

2 chicken breasts (slice into $1/2$ inch wide pieces)
1 red and 1 green pepper (medium size)
(de-seeded and cut into small pieces)
8 oz tin button mushrooms
1 small onion (finely sliced)
1 medium courgette (finely sliced)
1 small tin pineapple (sliced)
2 to 3 tablespoons vegetable oil
2 tablespoons tomato sauce
1 tablespoon cornflour
1 tablespoons vinegar
1 dessertspoon sugar

SPICY CHILLIE CRABS
(PENANG STYLE)

Cooking time: 25 minutes
Preparation time: 15 minutes

Serves 4

3 lbs (1.5 kilo) medium sized crabs
6 dried chillies (soaked in water until soft and drained)
10 small shallots (peeled and finely sliced)
1 inch (2.5 cm) prawn paste (blachan)
5 cloves garlic (peeled and chopped)
2 oz Buah Keras or also known as "candle nuts" or use cashew nuts
1 small tin salted brown soya bean
1/4 cup of water
5 tablespoons vegetable oil
2 large eggs

METHOD:

1. Wash crabs first, then chop them into halves if they are big. Pound or blend the chillies, prawn paste, shallots, garlic together into a smooth paste. Add a few drops of water to make it is easier to blend. Switch off and stir with a spatula.

2. Grind the candle nuts first before adding it to the blender.

3. Heat oil in a large wok until quite hot, add the paste and fry for 3 minutes until light brown. Then add the crabs and stir well for 10 to 15 minutes.

4. Add salted soya beans to the crabs, water and salt to taste. Stir for 1 minute and cover wok with a lid for 10 minutes, do not let it get dry. Add more water if necessary.

5. Crack 2 eggs into the crabs mixture and continue stirring. When cooked the crabs should be pink in colour. Serve with boiled rice.

TIPS:

Once the crabs are cooked, transfer into a large dish to serve. Use a hammer to break the crabs to get the meat out.

BLACK PEPPER CRABS
(PENANG STYLE)

Cooking time: 25 minutes
Preparation time: 15 minutes

Serves 4

1 lb 5 oz (600 g) fresh medium sized crabs
1 teaspoon fresh peppercorns -
1 tablespoon garlic (chopped)
5 chilli padis (chopped) small green chillies

SAUCE INGREDIENTS:

$1/2$ teaspoon salt
1 teaspoon sugar
$1/2$ teaspoon ground black pepper
$1^1/2$ teaspoons sesame oil
1 teaspoon Maggi fish sauce/ stock granules
1 tablespoon water
1 dessertspoon cornflour, mix with water into a cream

FOR GARNISH:

Chopped spring onions and coriander leaves

METHOD:

1. Wash and clean crabs. Cut into halves. Roast pepper corns and then crush.

2. Heat wok with oil when hot add the garlic and stir for 2 minutes until medium brown.

3. Add chilli padis and peppercorns.

4. Stir fry for 2 minutes and add the crabs. Then add the sauce ingredients.

5. Cover the wok with lid and let it boil for 10 to 15 minutes and then remove the lid and add the cornflour mixture. Simmer for 10 minutes and switch off.

6. Transfer into a large dish and garnish with spring onions and chopped coriander leaves.

TIPS:

Chilli padis are small green chillies which are very hot.

EGG CURRY
(INDIAN)

Cooking time : 15 minutes
Preparation time : 10 minutes

Serves 4

6 eggs (medium size)
2 tablespoons vegetable oil
1 medium size onion (finely sliced)
1 teaspoon salt
1 dessertspoon cornflour
1/2 teaspoon cummin seeds
1/2 teaspoon turmeric powder
1/2 teaspoon red chilli powder
5 cloves garlic (finely sliced)
1 teaspoon coriander powder
1 small tin tomato
2 or 3 green chillies (sliced into halves)
1/2 pint water
1 dessertspoon sugar
A few sprigs of coriander leaves for garnish (finely chopped)
2 tablespoons vegetable oil

METHOD:

1. Hard boil the eggs. Peel the shells and set aside. Wash and chop coriander leaves. Wash the chillies and slice into halves.

2. Heat a medium size saucepan with oil until quite hot, add the onions and stir for 1 to 2 minutes until light brown. Add all the spices, cornflour and stir well for a further 1 minute.

3. Then add the tomato and stir for 2 minutes. Add water, salt then sugar and let it boil for about 8 to 10 minutes over medium heat. Finally add the eggs, coriander leaves, chillies and simmer for 5 minutes . Taste to see if you need more salt or more chilli powder.

4. Serve with boiled rice and garnish with the rest of the coriander leaves.

AH CHAT EGG
(EGG SALAD PENANG STYLE)

Cooking Time: 15 minutes
Preparation Time: 5 minutes

Serves 4

2 cucumbers (cut into strips)
3 green chillies (cut into strips)
1 large onion (cut into quarters)
1 red and green chillies (pounded or blended)
4 cloves garlic (finely sliced)
1 teaspoon sugar
1 teaspoon vinegar
3 large eggs
A pinch of salt

METHOD:

1. Hard boil the eggs. Peel the eggs and cut into 4 quarters.

2. Heat saucepan with 1 tablespoon oil until hot add the blended chillies and garlic and stir fry for 2 minutes.

3. Add 1 cup of water, vinegar, sugar, onion, green and red chillies and salt to taste. Boil for 5 to 6 minutes.

4. Add the eggs then the cucumber and simmer for 5 minutes. Now it is ready to serve with boiled rice.

KAENG BHED PED YANG (SMOKED THAI DUCKLING CURRY)

Cooking time: 25 minutes
Preparation time: 10 minutes

Serves 4

1 smoked duckling or 4 pieces cooked chicken breasts or thighs
600 ml coconut milk
2 tablespoons curry paste
(made by mixing curry powder with a little water)
2 red and 2 green chillies (pounded or blended)
1 red or 1 green chilli (seeded and chopped)
(Use for garnishing)
2 tablespoons freshly chopped basil leaves
2 tablespoons cubed pineapple
(if tinned pineapple is used, drain the pineapple)
1 to 2 teaspoons soya sauce
A pinch of salt
A pinch of pepper
2 tablespoons vegetable oil

METHOD:

1. Heat the wok with oil. When hot, add the blended ingredients and stir for 2 minutes until oil separates from the chilli paste and switch off. Then heat the coconut milk for approximately 5 minutes on low heat and remove half the milk and put on one side for later.

2. Heat the remaining half of the milk. Add chicken /duckling pieces, then reduce the heat and simmer until chicken /duckling is tender. Add the soya sauce, the fried chilli paste and the rest of the milk, stirring well and simmer until the mixture is smooth and creamy.

3. Just before serving lightly saute the chopped chilli and sprinkle over the curry. Add the cubed pineapple and the chopped basil leaves. Add salt and pepper to taste. Serve curry on a bed of hot rice.

NASI KANDAR (PENANG STYLE) (INDIAN FISH CURRY)

Cooking time: 25 minutes
Preparation time: 15 minutes

Serves 4

8 small fish (mackerels or trout)
2 to 3 tablespoons vegetable or peanut oil
5 to 6 fresh red chillies (whole)
3 to 4 curry leaves
1 inch piece (2 cm) fresh ginger (sliced)
1 cup thick coconut milk

3 medium onions (sliced)
$1/2$ teaspoon salt
A pinch of sugar
1 packet fish curry powder (200 g)
1 dessertspoon aniseed powder (Jintan manis)
1 dessertspoon cummin powder (Jintan puteh)
1 cup Tamarind juice
1 cup of water
$1/2$ teaspoon turmeric powder
$1/2$ teaspoon red chilli powder

METHOD:

1. Soak tamarind fruit in a small cup of water for 10 minutes. Save juice for the curry and discard the stones.

2. Wash and gut the fish. Heat oil in a large saucepan, when the oil is quite hot, add the fresh red chillies and stir for 1 minute. Then add the curry leaves, ginger, onions and fry for 2 minutes. Add the turmeric, chilli powder and stir for 1 minute and switch off.

3. Mix the fish powder, aniseed powder, cumin powder together in a small bowl with 2 to 3 teaspoons of water until creamy. Add this mixture to the turmeric and chilli sauce and mix well together.

4. Boil the curry sauce for 2 to 3 minutes on medium heat, then add the tamarind juice and stir for 1 minute. Continue boiling for about 5 minutes, reduce heat add the coconut milk and stir frequently. Add 1 cup of water and continue boiling.

5. Next add all the fish and stir for 2 minutes, add salt and sugar to taste. Simmer for 10 to 15 minutes until fish is tender. Serve with boiled rice or biryani rice.

GRILLED PLAICE IN SPICY CHILLIES SAUCE

Cooking time: 35 minutes
Preparation time: 15 minutes

Serves 4

2 large plaice or trout
6 to 8 shallots (peeled)
1 inch (2.5 cm) piece blachan (prawn paste)
1 stick lemon grass (finely sliced)
2 inch (5 cm) fresh yellow ginger (peeled and finely sliced)
6 to 10 fresh or dried chillies
(if using dried chillies, soak in water until soft and drained)
2 to 3 tablespoons Tamarind juice
(soak Tamarind fruit in 1 cup of water for
for 10 minutes then drain the juice. Discard the stones).

METHOD:

1. Wash the plaice, slit open in the middle and gut. Then rinse and pat dry with kitchen paper. Set to one side.

2. Pound or blend the shallots, prawn paste (blachan), lemon grass, yellow ginger, red chillies into a smooth paste with a few drops of water. Blend for 1 to 2 minutes. Switch off and stir with a fork and set aside.

3. Put the plaice in an oval dish and add the paste and mix well. Then add 2 to 3 tablespoons of tamarind juice and stir for 1 to 2 minutes.

4. Then put the plaice onto a tin foil, make a parcel and seal. Grill under the grill for 15 to 20 minutes until cooked. After grilling check to see if it is cooked, if not grill for a further 5 to 10 minutes.

5. It can also be cooked in the oven for 35 minutes on Gas Mark 4 on 350° F/ 180° C.

TIPS:
Use 5 to 6 chillies if you prefer it mild.
Tamarind fruit is sold in small packet and so is blachan (prawn paste). It is sold in Indian or Chinese supermarkets.

FISH SARDINE
(PHILIPPINE STYLE)

Cooking time: 20 minutes
Preparation time: 10 minutes

Serves 4

4 medium sized sardines
2 to 3 cloves garlic (chopped)
1 medium onion (finely sliced)
1 inch piece ginger 2.5 cm (finely slice)

2 tablespoons vinegar (white or brown)
1 to 2 tablespoons fish sauce

METHOD:

1. Cut heads off fish, gut and clean them. Prepare the ingredients in a bowl for a marinade and mix well. Put fish into a pyrex and cover with lid and marinate for 1 hour.

2. If using vinegar do not add water.

3. Cook on Gas Mark 4 350° F/180° C for about 15 to 20 minutes until fish is tender.

Garnish with fresh sliced onions on top of fish, fresh sliced tomatoes and lemon wedges. Serve with boiled rice.

FRIED THAI FISH

Cooking time: 15 minutes
Preparation time: 10 minutes

Serves 4

2 fish (675 g) or 1¹/₂ Trout or Mackerel
1 tablespoon ginger (finely sliced)
3 red chillies (finely sliced)
3 green chillies (finely sliced)
1 medium onion (finely sliced)

INGREDIENTS TO BE BLENDED:

100 g dried prawns (4 oz)soaked in
water for 5 minutes until soft and drained
6 small shallots (finely sliced)
3 cloves garlics (finely sliced)
1/2 yellow ginger or 1/2 teaspoon turmeric powder
6 dried chillies (soaked in water until soft and drained)

SOUP:

1 tablespoon fish soya sauce
1 tablespoon sugar
2 tablespoons vinegar
A pinch of Aji-no-moto
3 tablespoons vegetable oil

METHOD:

1. Wash and gut the fish and rub with a tablespoon of salt. Then rinse.

2. After cleaning rub with another 1/2 a teaspoon of salt and set aside.

3. Heat the wok with oil until quite hot. Add the fish and fry until it is reddish brown in colour, turning over. It should take about 7 to 8 minutes each side.

4. Put the fish onto an oval shape shallow plate. Arrange salad round the plate.

5. Then stir fry the blended ingredients 2 to 3 minutes then add fresh chillies, onions and soup and stir for 1 minute and pour over the fish.

FRIED SHARK'S FINS

Cooking time: 25 minutes
Preparation time: 15 minutes

Serves 4

150 g (5 oz) shark's fins
1 small tin crab meat
75 g bamboo shoots
75 g lean roasted pork (Chinese Char Siew)
2 spring onions (finely sliced
4 oz (100g) ham (sliced)
6 eggs
1/2 teaspoon salt
1/2 white wine
A pinch of pepper
2 to 3 tablespoons vegetable oil

METHOD:

1. Wash the spring onions and finely slice. Wash and clean the shark's fins.

2. Roast the lean pork in oven for 20 to 25 minutes or put under the grill until cooked.

3. Crack 6 eggs into a bowl. Put finely sliced roasted pork, crab meat and shark's fins into the egg mixture.

4. Heat the wok with oil until quite hot on medium heat. Pour in enough egg mixture to cover the pan and cook for 10 to 12 minutes each side.

2. Sprinkle with salt, pepper and garlic powder. Grill the lobsters for a few minutes on either side to get a nice light brown colour. Transfer the lobsters onto four plates and decorate with tomatoes, cucumber, lettuce and prawn crackers.

3. Peel potatoes and cut into finger size and deep fry in hot oil until crispy. Remove the chips from the fryer and put onto a plate covered with kitchen paper.

   Serve with chips or fried rice. Pour the dressings over the lobsters and garnish with slices of lemon. Also serve with chilli sauce.

CLAMS WITH MANGO

Cooking time: 15 minutes
Preparation time: 10 minutes

Serves 4

1 lb clams (450 g) with shells
1 medium size mango
1 to 2 tablespoon vegetable oil
1 fresh red chilli (finely sliced)
1 to 2 cloves garlic (chopped)
1 teaspoon light soya sauce

METHOD:

1. Wash clams several times and drain.

2. Peel and slice mango and cut into 1 inch cubes.

3. Heat wok until hot, add oil and garlic and stir-fry until light brown. Add clams (with shells on) and stir for 8 to 10 minutes until shells are opened.

4. Add mango and chillies and stir for a further 3 to 4 minutes then add soya sauce. Serve with rice.

SQUID STUFFED WITH RICE

Cooking time: 30 minutes
Preparation time: 10 minutes

Serves 4

8 medium sized squids (3.5 inches long)
2 cups rice (washed and drained)
2 cups of Dashi soup
1 teaspoon salt
1/3 cup of soya sauce
1 1/2 tablespoons sugar
2 tablespoons Japanese Wine (Sake)
1/2 teaspoon Aji-no-moto (gourmet powder)

METHOD:

1. Wash squids cut off the long hands. Stuff each squid with washed rice, making sure all parts are closed, by stitching them together with little bamboo sticks.

2. Boil 2 cups of dashi soup with salt in a big shallow pan, and lay the 8 squids flat and cook for 20 minutes over medium heat.

3. After you have cooked the soup, add Sake, sugar and soya sauce and boil once and reduce the heat and continue cooking for another 10 minutes. Serve squids with the remainder of the soup.

GRILLED SQUIDS IN SPICY CHILLI SAUCE

Cooking time: 25 minutes
Preparation time: 15 minutes

Serves 4

2 lb (900 g) fresh squids
6 to 8 shallots (peeled)
1 inch 2.5 cm piece blachan (prawn paste)
1 stick lemon grass (finely sliced)
2 inch (5 cm) fresh yellow ginger (peeled and finely sliced)
6 to 10 red fresh chillies or dried (if dried soak in water until soft and drained)
2 to 3 tablespoons tamarind juice (soak Tamarind fruit in 1 cup of water for 10 minutes and then drained the juice. Discard the stones).

METHOD:

1. Wash squid and take out the hard bits in the middle. Then cut the squid into rings about 1/2 inch wide. Cut the tentacles into 2 inch lengths.

2. Pound or blend the shallots, blachan, lemon grass, yellow ginger, red chillies into a smooth paste with a few drops of water. Blend for 2 minutes. Switch off and stir with a spatula and set aside.

3. Put the squid into a bowl and add the paste and mix together. Then add 2 to 3 tablespoons of tamarind juice and stir for 1 to 2 minutes.

4. Place the squid onto the tin foil and make into a big parcel and seal. Put under the grill for 15 to 20 minutes, or cook in the oven for 30 minutes on Gas Mark 4 on 350° F/ 180° C.

5. After cooking, open and check to see if it is cooked. If not allow for a further 5 to 10 minutes. Serve with boiled rice.

TIPS:
Use 5 to 6 chillies if you prefer it mild.
Tamarind fruit is sold in small packet and so is blachan (prawn paste). It is sold in Indian or Chinese supermarkets.

DEEP FRIED SQUIDS
SOTONG (PENANG STYLE)

Cooking time: 20 minutes
Preparation time: 8 minutes

Serves 4

8 oz (225 g) squids
A pinch of salt
4 teaspoons curry powder
A pinch of pepper
6 oz (175 g) cornflour
1 litre oil for deep-frying

METHOD:

1. Wash and dry the squids. Add salt, curry powder and pepper and marinate for 15 minutes.

2. Then coat with flour on both sides.

3. Heat wok with enough oil until quite hot, deep fry the squids for about 7 to 8 minutes turning over until medium brown. Serve with rice and salad.

TIPS:
This dish is quite spicy. If you like it hot, add more curry powder.
Squids also known as "Sotong" in Malayan language.

TO-FU WITH PRAWNS

Cooking time: 10 minutes
Preparation time: 15 minutes

Serves 2

2 pieces of white To-Fu (bean curd)
1 cup of water
8 oz (225 g) fresh prawns or cooked prawns
1 dessertspoon oyster sauce
1 dessertspoon light soya sauce
2 tablespoons vegetable oil or peanut oil
5 cloves garlic (chopped)
1 spring onion (cut into 2 inch length)
A pinch of salt

METHOD:

1. Cut each To-Fu into four pieces. Wash and peel prawns. Heat wok with 2 tablespoons of oil until quite hot, add the garlic and stir for about 2 minutes.

2. Add the prawns and stir fry for 2 to 3 minutes, then add the To-Fu and stir fry for 2 to 3 minutes.

3. Add the spring onions, oyster sauce, light soya sauce and water and simmer for 2 to 3 minutes. Add salt to taste. Transfer into a serving dish and serve with boiled rice.

TIPS:
White To-Fu is sold in cartons in local supermarkets. It is very soft and delicate and easy to cut.

PRAWN SAMBAL
(MALAYAN SPICY PRAWN)

Cooking time: 20 minutes
Preparation time: 15 minutes

3 to 4 tablespoons vegetable oil
2 tablespoons brown sugar
1 teaspoon salt
3 tablespoons thick coconut milk
4 tablespoons lime juice
1 lb (450 g) medium sized prawns (peeled and de-veined)

CHILLI PASTE:

10 fresh red chillies
3 medium red onions (peeled)
$2^1/_2$ cm (1 inch) galangal or "lengkuas" in Malay language
10 cloves garlic (peeled)
3 candlenuts or cashew nuts

METHOD:

1. Chop up all the ingredients for chilli paste. Then put in blender and blend into a smooth paste. Add a little water to help it blend. Switch off and use a fork to stir or to get it out.

2. Heat 2 tablespoons of oil in the wok until quite hot, add the paste and stir for 3 to 4 minutes until oil separates from the paste.

3. Then add brown sugar, salt and coconut milk and bring to the boil. Add lime juice and prawns and simmer for 8 to 10 minutes until prawns are cooked. Add more oil if necessary. Taste to see if you need more salt. Serve with boiled rice. Pineapples can be added to the prawns.

TIPS:
This is a very hot and spicy dish, if you like it mild use about 5 chillies.

SAVOURY PRAWNS

Cooking time: 15 to 20 minutes
Preparation time: 10 minutes

600 g medium size prawns (1 lb 5 oz)
6 fresh red chillies (de-seeded) and finely sliced
2 buah keras (candle nuts) or use cashew nuts
Ground the nuts
1 teaspoon turmeric or 1 inch piece fresh yellow ginger (finely sliced)
6 dessertspoons vegetable oil

METHOD:

1. Wash the prawns, remove heads and shells and leave tails on. Slit prawns in the middle.

2. Blend the red chillies, nuts, turmeric and ginger together to make a paste.

3. Mix the prawns with the paste and salt in a bowl.

4. Heat the wok with oil until quite hot, add the prawns and fry for about 15 to 20 minutes until prawns turn pink in colour. It is now ready to serve.

TIPS:

"Buah Keras" is a Malayan word and is also known as "Kimiri" in Indonesia.
"Yellow ginger" is also known as "Kunyit" in Malayan word.

KERABU ASAM
(CUCUMBER SALAD)

Preparation time : 15 minutes

1 medium cucumber
1 large onion (cut into rings)

2 teaspoons lime juice
1 teaspoon blended dried prawns or pounded
2 teaspoons sambal blachan (prawn paste)
1/4 teaspoon salt
1 teaspoon sugar

METHOD:

1. Wash cucumber and diced.

2. Blend or pound the dried prawns.

3. Put cucumber and prawns into a large bowl with onions and lime juice and mix well. Then add prawn paste, salt and sugar to taste. This is use as a side dish.

ASAM PRAWNS

Cooking time: 15 to 20 minutes
Preparation time: 10 minutes

Serves 4

1 lb (450 g) medium size prawns
2 cups coconut milk (santan)
1/4 cup tamarind juice
1 teaspoon salt
1 teaspoon sugar
A pinch of Aji-no-moto
1/2 cup vegetable oil

INGREDIENTS TO BE BLENDED:

15 small shallots (peeled and finely sliced)
1 stalk lemon grass (serai) finely sliced
10 dried chillies (soaked in water until soft and drained)
2 fresh lengkuas (finely sliced) if using dried ones
soaked in water until soft for 30 to 40 minutes
1/2 teaspoon turmeric powder or fresh yellow ginger 1 inch
2 cm piece of blachan (prawn paste)
1 teaspoon coriander seed (sauted)

METHOD:

1. Wash the prawns. Leave the shells on including heads and tails. Blend the ingredients that is shallots, lemon grass, chillies, lengkuas and prawn paste.

2. Heat the wok until quite hot add the oil and then add the paste. Stir for 2 to 3 minutes until oil separates from the paste. Add the turmeric and coriander and stir for 1 minute.

3. Then reduce heat and add the coconut milk and keep stirring for 3 minutes.

4. Add the tamarind juice, salt, sugar, aji-no-moto and boil for 5 minutes.

5. Next add the prawns and stir-fry for 5 to 6 minutes until the colour turns pink. Now it is ready to serve with rice. This dish gives a really nice sweet and sour taste.

TIPS:
Lengkuas is part of the ginger family. It is sold in a dried packet already sliced which takes time to soak until very soft. Fresh ones are available in Chinese supermarkets.
Tamarind is a sweet and sour fruit available dried in a packet. You will only need a small amount of fruit soaked in water. Keep the juice for cooking. Discard the stones.

PRAWN IN GARLIC SAUCE

Cooking time: 20 minutes
Preparation time: 15 minutes

Serves : 4

1 lb (450 gm) king prawns
4 oz (100 gm) butter
5 cloves garlic (chopped)
A pinch of black pepper
A pinch of salt
1 dessertspoon sugar
2 tablespoons peanut oil or vegetable oil

METHOD:

1. Wash prawns first and peel the shells. Heat the wok with the oil when hot add the prawns and stir fry for 10 to 15 minutes. Turn off heat. When prawns are cooked they should be pink in colour.

GARLIC SAUCE:

2. Melt the butter in the saucepan for 2 minutes then add the garlic until light brown. Add all the ingredients and stir over medium heat for 2 minutes. Turn off heat.

3. Transfer the prawns into a dish and pour the garlic sauce over the prawns. Serve with boiled rice or fried rice.

SPICY CHILLIE PRAWNS
SAMBAI HAI BEE (PENANG STYLE)

Cooking time: 20 minutes
Preparation time: 15 minutes

Serves 4

8 oz dried prawns (225 g) soaked in water until soft
6 to 8 dried red chillies (soaked in water until soft)
6 to 8 shallots (peeled)
1 stick lemon grass (chopped)
1/4 cup tamarind juice
2 tablespoons vegetable or peanut oil
1 dessertspoon sugar

METHOD:

1. Soak tamarind fruit in a small bowl for 10 to 15 minutes. Use the juice for cooking and discard the stones. Once the prawns are soft, drain and set aside. When the chillies are soft, drain and set aside.

2. Pound or blend the chillies, shallots, lemon grass into a smooth paste. Add a few drops of water to make it easier to blend. Switch off and transfer into a bowl.

3. Pound or blend the prawns for 2 to 3 minutes. If the blender is not big enough to put all the prawns in, you might have to repeat 2 or 3 times more.

4. Heat the wok with oil until hot, add the paste first, stir for 2 to 3 minutes. Then add all the prawns and stir for 5 to 6 minutes. Add tamarind juice and sugar and stir again for 5 minutes until prawns are cooked and the juice is reduced.

TIPS:
This is a very spicy dish. Serve with boiled rice, cucumber and pineapple.
If you prefer it mild, use only 4 to 5 chillies. Tamarind fruit is available in Indian supermarkets and also Chinese supermarkets.

VEGETABLE AND PRAWN CURRY (MALAYSIAN STYLE)

Cooking time : 20 minutes
Preparation time : 10 minutes

Serves 4

300 g (9 oz) French beans
125 g (4 oz) medium size prawns
1 cup coconut milk
$1/2$ cup of thick coconut milk
2 tablespoons vegetable or peanut oil
A pinch of salt

TO MAKE PASTE:

Ingredients:

2 large fresh red chillies (seeded)
4 candle nuts or cashew nuts also known as " buah keras" in Malay language
2 slices of lengkuas or galangal or 2 teaspoons of laos powder
1 thick slice fresh yellow ginger or 1 teaspoon turmeric powder
$1/2$ teaspoon dried shrimp paste (blachan) or prawn paste
8 small shallots or onions

METHOD:

1. Wash and cut french beans into 3 cm in lengths. Shell and de-vein the prawns leaving tails on.

2. Blend the chillies, candle nuts, lengkuas, yellow ginger, shrimp paste, onions together until smooth. Add a little water if necessary. Switch off and stir with a fork.

3. Heat oil in medium saucepan, when hot add the paste ingredients and stir-fry for about 2 to 3 minutes. Add prawns and stir for 5 minutes.

4. Then reduce the heat and add half a cup of thick coconut milk and stir for 2 to 3 minutes. When prawns turn pink colour, add French beans and salt and stir for 1 minute.

5. Add the rest of the coconut milk, stir again and simmer for 10 minutes. Taste to see if more salt is needed.

TIPS:
Any vegetable can be use instead of beans. This is a very spicy dish serve with boiled rice and vegetable salad.

RICE COOKED IN COCONUT MILK WITH SPICY PRAWNS
NASI LEMAK (PENANG STYLE)

Cooking time: 35 minutes
Preparation time: 25 minutes

Serves 2

2 cups of long grain rice
1 cup thick coconut milk
1 cup of water
5 shallots (peeled and sliced)
5 dried red chillies (soak in hot water until soft and drain)
1 inch piece (2.5 cm) prawn paste (blachan)
8 anchovies
6 oz (175 g) fresh prawns (unpeeled)
1/2 cucumber (finely sliced)
2 to 3 tablespoons tamarind juice
1 tablespoon dark soya sauce
2 tablespoons vegetable or peanut oil

METHOD:

1. Soak tamarind fruit with 1/2 cup of water in a small bowl for 10 minutes. Save the juice for cooking. Discard the stones. Wash rice and boil with the coconut milk and water for 25 minutes until soft and fluffy.

2. Grill the prawn paste until brown on both sides for 2 to 3 minutes and cut into small pieces. Pound or blend the chillies, shallots, blachan for 2 minutes with a few drops of water until the paste is smooth. Switch off and stir with a spatula.

3. Heat the wok with oil until quite hot, add the prawns and stir fry for 5 to 6 minutes. Add soya sauce and tamarind juice and stir for 2 to 3 minutes until brown in colour.

4. Heat oil in another frying pan when hot, add anchovies and stir fry for 4 to 5 minutes each side until cooked.

WRAPPING A PARCEL:

Use a tin foil 10" x 10" square, add 2 tablespoons of the cooked rice in the middle of the parcel, then add 4 to 5 cooked prawns and 4 to 5 cooked anchovies with a small amount of chillies on one side. Add a few slices of cucumber and fold into a parcel. Serve hot.

The chilli paste is quite hot. If you like it mild use 2 to 3 chillies. Once wrapped in parcel it can be eaten hot or cold. Or it can be warmed up later in oven.
Prawn paste is available in Chinese Supermarkets.

2. Wash the cabbage and cut into 1 inch wide pieces. Wash spring onions and cut diagonally into 1/2 inch wide pieces. If using fresh prawns, peel off the skins and hairs and cut off the head leaving the tails on. De-vein the prawns by cutting the middle part open and take out the grey string.

3. Heat the wok until hot add oil then add garlic and stir until light brown. Then add the prawns and stir for 2 minutes. Add the cabbage and spring onions and stir for 1 minute. Add dark soya sauce, Indonesian sweet soya sauce and sesame oil and stir frequently.

4. Next add the Bee Hoon noodles and stir until well mixed for 5 to 6 minutes. Add more soya sauce, salt and pepper to taste.   Garnish with golden crispy fried onions on top.

INDONESIAN MEE GORENG
(STIR FRIED NOODLES)

Cooking time : 20 minutes
Preparation time: 15 to 20 minutes

Serves 4

2 lb (1 kilo) fresh or dried egg noodles
8 oz (225) sprouts
1 large carrot (peeled and finely sliced)
5 cloves of garlic (chopped)
1 dessertspoon sesame oil
3 tablespoons vegetable oil or peanut oil
2 tablespoons dark soya sauce
1 tablespoon (Indonesian sweet soya sauce)
1 or 2 eggs (beaten)
1 dessertspoon chilli sauce (optional)
1 teaspoon light soya sauce
2 lemons for garnish (cut each lemon into 4 quarters)
A few lettuce leaves (finely sliced)
2 or 3 onions (finely sliced)
3 tomatoes (sliced)
1/2 cucumber (finely sliced)
1 packet of krupuk (prawn crackers)

METHOD:

1. Wash all vegetables and slice. Deep fry the onions until golden brown for garnish and
    set aside to cool. Boil the noodles for 8 to 10 minutes until soft, drained and put on
    one side.

2. Heat 2 tablespoons of oil in the wok until quite hot, add the garlic and stir fry for 2
    minutes until light brown. Add the carrots and cabbages and stir for 3 minutes, then
    add the noodles and stir until well mixed.

3. Add the dark soya sauce, sweet soya sauce and the light sauce and stir frequently for
    3 minutes until noodles are brown. Add sesame oil and continue stirring. Then add the
    chilli sauce and stir again.

4. Make a well in the centre of the wok and add 1 dessertspoon of oil, wait for 1 minute
    then pour the egg into the middle. After 1 minute stir the noodles until well mix and
    transfer onto a serving dish.
    Sprinkle crispy onions over the noodles. Garnish with lemon wedges and lettuce leaves.
    Serve with tomato, cucumber slices and krupuk (prawn crackers).

TIPS:
If using fresh noodles there's no need to boil.

SOMEN
(JAPANESE NOODLES)

Cooking time: 10 minutes
Preparation time: 15 minutes

4 Servings

A pack of 4 Somen dry noodles
A few spring onions (minced)
Some horesradish paste
Some fish paste or sliced ham
6 to 8 Chinese mushrooms or anything you like

DIPPING SAUCE:

2 cups of Dashi soup
1 tablespoon soya sauce
1 teaspoon salt
1/2 teaspoon sugar
A pinch of Aji-no-moto

Boil all the above ingredients once and cool. Keep in refrigerator. Serve this into 4 small serving dishes.

METHOD:

1. Prepare the dipping soup first. Put 2 cups of Dashi soup in a small saucepan with 1 tablespoon of soya sauce and 1 teaspoon of salt, half a teaspoon of sugar and a pinch of aji-no-moto. Boil once and cool. Keep in refrigerator.

2. Boil the Somen noodles for about 3 minutes, then drain, and rinse with cold water. Put some cold water and some ice cubes onto the glass bowl and add cold Somen into this.

3. Minced the spring onions and some Japanese horseradish paste. The radish is a "must" which is served with the Somen noodles. You can add some fish paste (sliced) or ham, cooked or Chinese mushrooms (cooked).

4. Dip Somen into the dashi soup add the above ingredients of your choice and enjoy this typical Summer recipe.

INDIAN VEGETABLE RICE

Cooking Time : 30 minutes
Preparation : 10 minutes

Serves 4 to 5

2 cups Basmati rice
1/2 lb (225 g) potatoes (finely sliced diagonally)
4 oz (112 g) peas
1 large carrot (peeled and finely sliced)
4 dessertspoons vegetable oil
1 1/2 teaspoons salt
1 1/2 to 2 medium size onions (peeled and finely sliced)
1/2 teaspoon cummin seeds
3 cups water
1/3 teaspoon turmeric
1 small jar natural yoghurt

METHOD:

1. Wash rice and soak for 20 to 30 minutes. Peel and finely slice potatoes.

2. Heat the oil in a saucepan and add onions. When onions are brown add potatoes, carrots, and fry for 5 minutes, then add peas, salt, turmeric, cummin seeds and fry for a further 2 to 3 minutes.

3. Add water, during boiling add the rice and cook on a medium heat for about 25 to 30 minutes until rice is soft and fluffy and the vegetables are tender. Serve with natural yogurt and curry.

GOMOKU GOHAN
(RICE)

Cooking time: 25 minutes
Preparation time: 20 minutes

4 Servings

* 5 dried Chinese mushrooms (medium)
  soaked in 1 1/2 cups of water until soft
* 1 medium carrot
* 300 g bamboo shoots
* 100 g dried shrimps
* 80 g green peas
3 cups of rice
3 cups of water
1/2 teaspoon salt
2 tablespoons soya sauce
1 teaspoon sugar
1 tablespoonful Japanese Wine Sake
1 teaspoon of salt

METHOD:

1. Wash 3 cups of rice with 3 cups of water and then soak in water with 1/2 teaspoon of salt and leave to soak for at least 20 minutes.

2. Chop all the vegetables into small pieces, except prawns and peas and boil for 5 minutes in a medium saucepan.

3. Use 1 1/2 cups of the mushroom water and add 2 tablespoons of soya sauce, 1 teaspoon of sugar, 1 tablespoon of Japanese Sake and 1 teaspoon of salt and boil for 5 minutes in another small saucepan.

4. After all these have been boiled there should still be some soup left over. About 1/2 a cup of this soup is use for cooking Gomoku Rice.

5. Cook rice with 1/2 a cup of mushroom soup and 2 1/2 cups of water until rice is soft and fluffy. Reduce heat and simmer for 25 minutes and switch off.

6. Leave rice to settle for at least 10 minutes. Then mix rice with the vegetables and shrimps ingredients and serve.

TIPS:

In Japan odd numbers (except 9) are preferred to even numbers. Even numbers are divided up and this means separation, which is used in funerals. So in GOMOKU GOHAN, ingredients are usually five, for GO means five in Japanese. You can choose 5 types of vegetables. GOMOKU GOHAN means rice with 5 kinds of ingredients. It is classed as rather special but not prepared on special occasions.

TOMATO RICE
(PENANG STYLE)

Cooking time: 25 minutes
Preparation time: 5 minutes

Serves 4

4 cups long grain rice
2 to 3 cinnamon sticks
2 tablespoons ghee
1 dessert spoons cardamon pods.
2 Pandan leaves (optional)
5 to 6 tablespoons tomato sauce

METHOD:

1. Wash Pandan leaves and drain. Tie them into a knot separately. Wash rice and rinse twice.

2. Heat a large saucepan with the ghee for 2 minutes, add cardamon pods and cinnamon sticks and stir for 2 minutes. Then add tomato sauce, rice and enough water to cover rice. Boil rice for 25 minutes until soft and fluffy. Serve with curry sauce.

TIPS:

Pandan leaves are use for aroma and small amount of juice are use for colouring especially for making cakes.   Pandan leaves are sold in Chinese supermarkets. If Pandan leaves are not available use 2 bay leaves.   One cup of rice is enough for one person.

INDONESIAN STIR FRIED RICE

Cooking time: 25 minutes
Preparation time: 15 minutes

Serves 4

4 cups of long grain rice
1 medium onion (finely sliced)
8 oz (225 g) chicken breasts or prawns
1 medium size egg
4 oz (112 g) carrot (finely sliced)
4 oz (112 g) peas (optional)
1 small green and red pepper (cut into small pieces)
1 medium onion (finely sliced)
5 cloves of garlic (chopped)
1/2 teaspoon salt
1 dessertspoon tomato sauce
1 dessertspoon chilli sauce
2 tablespoons Indonesian soya sauce
1 fresh red chilli (finely sliced)
3 to 4 tablespoons vegetable oil
A sprinkle of light soya sauce
2 spring onions (chopped)
1 packet of prawn crackers

METHOD:

1. Wash rice and boil for 25 minutes until soft and fluffy. When it is cooked, leave for 10 minutes to settle. Heat the wok with 2 tablespoons of oil until quite hot, add the onions and garlic and stir fry until light brown.

2. Add the chicken and stir for 2 to 3 minutes, then add the vegetables and stir for 2 minutes. Add Indonesian soya sauce, light soya sauce, tomato sauce and stir for 2 minutes. Add the rice and stir until well mixed.

3. Boil peas for 3 minutes and drain. Add to the rice and stir for 2 minutes. Make a well in the centre of the wok and add 1 dessertspoon oil and crack an egg in it. Wait for 1 minute and stir the rice until well mixed.

4. Transfer rice onto a large dish and sprinkle spring onions on top. Served with prawn crackers, a few slices of cucumber, tomato and chilli sauce.

FRIED RICE
(TAIWANESE STYLE)

Cooking time : 35 minutes
Preparation time: 10 minutes

Serves 4

4 cups of Basmati rice or long grain rice
4 cups of water
2 to 3 tablespoons vegetable oil
A few spring onions (cut into 1 inch length)
1 large egg
8 oz (225 g) cooked or fresh prawns or
8 oz (225 g) lean pork (finely sliced)
A pinch salt
A pinch of pepper

METHOD:

1. Wash the rice until the water is clear. Boil rice with 4 cups of water in a medium saucepan or rice cooker. It takes about 25 minutes to cook and then let it settle for 10 minutes.

2. Heat wok until quite hot add oil, then add shrimps or pork and stir fry for 10 minutes, add the spring onions and stir again for 1 minute.

3. Next add the rice and stir fry until well mixed for 5 to 6 minutes, add salt and pepper to taste.

4. Finally make a well in the middle of the wok and add 1 dessertspoon of oil and then crack an egg into the centre for 1 minute and then stir it all together until well mixed.

5. Now it is ready to serve. Add chillies if you like it spicy.

BIRYANI RICE
(YELLOW RICE)

Cooking time: 25 minutes
Preparation time: 15 minutes

Serves 2

1 packet masala biryani spice powder
2 oz (50 g) ghee
2 cups rice
1 medium carrot (finely sliced)
1 small green and red pepper (cut into small pieces)
1 medium onion (finely sliced)
$1/2$ teaspoon salt
8 to 10 cardamon pods
5 cloves of garlic (chopped)
2 curry leaves

METHOD:

1. Wash vegetables first before cutting. Wash rice and rinse twice. Heat a large saucepan with ghee until it melts, then add masala Biryani powder and stir fry for 2 minutes until brown. Add the rice and enough water to cover it and boil for 25 minutes until soft and fluffy.

2. During cooking add all the mixed vegetables and stir, then add cardamon pods, garlic and curry leaves and stir again.

4. Add salt to taste. Serve with curry dishes.

TIPS:

1 cup of rice is enough for 1 person. So if you are cooking for 4 persons you need 4 cups of rice.

CHICK PEAS SALAD (CHANNA CHAT)
(SIDE DISH)

Cooking Time: 30 minutes

Serves 4 to 6

2 cups chick peas
6 cups water
1 teaspoon salt
1/2 teaspoon red chilli (finely sliced)
2 green chillies (finely sliced)
3 medium size potatoes (peel and diced)
3 teaspoons plain yogurt

METHOD:

1. Soak chick peas overnight or at least for 4 to 6 hours.

2. Put water, chick peas, salt and red chillies into pressure cooker and cook for about 30 minutes. When chick peas are tender, strain them.

3. Boil potatoes separately in another saucepan.

4. Put chick peas and potatoes into a large bowl add a pinch of salt and red chillies, green chillies and yogurt. Mix all the ingredients thoroughly and it is ready to be served. It is not hot but spicy. This is only a side dish.

VEGETABLE TEMPURA
(JAPANESE STYLE)

Cooking time: 25 minutes
Preparation time: 20 minutes

Serves 4

8 oz (225 g) medium prawns
or 8 oz (225 g) chicken breasts
1 egg plant (aubergine) finely sliced
1 large carrot (cut into 3 to 4 inch long strips)
1 large onion (finely sliced into rings)
2 to 3 oz (60 g) french long beans
1 litre oil for deep frying

METHOD:

1. Wash prawns, pat dry with kitchen paper towel and leave tails on. Make a slit along the body to prevent curling during cooking. Cut the chicken into bite size pieces.

2. Wash all the vegetables. Finely slice green beans to about 4 inches in length. Finely slice the egg plant and cut the carrots.

TO MAKE TEMPURA BATTER:

5 oz (150 g) plain flour (sifted 2 or 3 times)
1 medium egg
A pinch of salt
2 cups of chilled water from the refrigerator

1. Put chilled water in a jug, then add the flour, salt and an egg and stir with a fork lightly. But do not stir too much. Dip each vegetable individually into the batter.

2. Heat the wok with oil until quite hot and deep fry the vegetables for 2 to 3 minutes, turning them over until medium brown. Remove the vegetables and put onto a paper towel to absorb the oil.

3. Dip the chicken and prawns in the batter and deep fry them for 2 to 3 minutes until medium brown and turn over. Remove meat and vegetables and put onto paper towel to absorb the oil.

    Decorate a large dish with prawns and vegetables and serve with Tempura dipping sauce.

TO MAKE DIPPING SAUCE:

1 packet of Dashi powder (mix with 2 cups of water)
$1/3$ teaspoon of salt
$1 1/2$ teaspoon of dark soya sauce
A pinch of aji-no-moto
1 tablespoon Japanese Wine (Sake)
$1/2$ teaspoon of sugar

First prepare the dipping sauce. Put 2 cups of dashi soup into a small saucepan.
Add all the ingredients and boil for about 8 minutes. This is use for dipping the meat.
Transfer the sauce into small bowls.

TIPS:

Tempura is a very famous Japanese dish. It can be found in most restaurants in Japan.
Some grated "radish" is a must to the dipping sauce.

CAULIFLOWER AND POTATOES
(PUNJAB DISTRICT)

Cooking Time: 29 minutes
Preparation Time: 10 minutes

Serves 4

1 medium cauliflower (cut into small pieces)
2 medium potatoes (peeled and cut into 8)
1 large onion (finely chopped)
1/2 teaspoon red chilli powder
1/2 to 1 teaspoon salt
1 teaspoon garam masala
4 cloves garlic (finely sliced)
1 inch ginger 2.5 cm (finely sliced)
1 fresh tomato (medium or large) finely sliced
3 tablespoons vegetable oil
1/2 cup water
1 teaspoon plain yogurt

METHOD:

1. Heat oil in large saucepan on medium heat, when hot add onions and stir fry until light brown. Then add chilli powder, salt, garam masala, garlic and ginger and a little bit water and yogurt and stir fry for 5 to 6 minutes.

2. Add tomato and stir again for 5 minutes then add cauliflower and potatoes and continue stirring for a further 2 to 3 minutes.

3. Next add 1/2 cup of water and cover with lid and cook on low heat for 10 to 15 minutes until vegetables are soft.

4. Serve with naan bread or chappatti.

MIXED VEGETABLE CURRY
(INDIAN STYLE)

Cooking time : 20 minutes
Preparation time : 15 minutes

2 medium onion (finely sliced)
$1/4$ teaspoon turmeric
2 tablespoons vegetable oil
1 teaspoon coriander powder
1 clove garlic (peeled and chopped)
1 small tin tomato
1 inch (2.5 cm) fresh ginger (finely sliced)
$1/2$ teaspoon cummin seeds
1 small jar natural yoghurt
2 inch piece cinnamon stick
2 to 3 green chillies (finely sliced)
4 oz (100 g) green beans or peas
1 teaspoon salt
1 small cauliflower (cut into florets)
2 medium size carrots (peeled and finely sliced)
1 small cabbage (finely sliced)
$1/2$ teaspoon red chilli powder
$1^{1}/2$ cups of water

For Garnish: Use a few sprigs of fresh chopped coriander leaves

METHOD:

1. Wash and slice all vegetables. Heat a deep medium size saucepan with oil until quite hot, add the onions and stir fry until medium brown.

2. Then add the ginger and garlic and stir for 2 minutes. Add the ground coriander and cummin seeds and stir for 1 minute. After 3 minutes add salt, red chilli powder, turmeric, tomatoes and green chillies.

3. Stir fry for 5 minutes, reduce heat and add 2 to 3 tablespoons of yoghurt and stir for 5 minutes.

4. Finally add all the vegetables and $1\frac{1}{2}$ cups of water and boil for 10 minutes. During cooking add fresh coriander leaves for garnish and stir. Use more salt if necessary.

KIMPIRA
(BURDOCK AND CARROTS)

Cooking Time: 17 minutes
Preparation Time : 10 minutes

Serves 4

2 long burdocks (long thin brown vegetable)
2 medium size carrots
1 tablespoon sesame oil
Some salad oil
A pinch of salt
A pinch of sugar
A tablespoon Japanese Wine (Sake)
$1\frac{1}{2}$ tablespoon soya sauce
1 red pepper (de-seeded and finely sliced)
A pinch of Aji-no-moto (Gourmet Powder)

METHOD:

1. Wash burdocks and carrots, peel and slice them (in the way you sharpen pencils) to 1.7 inches long and about $\frac{1}{3}$ inches wide. Put burdock into water for a while to remove the harshness then drain later.

2. Put oil in the frying pan and heat. Put burdocks and carrots into the pan and stir fry for about 10 minutes until they are 90% cooked.

3. Add red pepper, sugar, salt, sake and soya sauce and stir fry. Then add sesame oil and mix well. Finish with a pinch of Aji-no-moto.

TIPS:

If Burdock is not available, use parsnip for substitute. But there is no need to soak into water.
Burdock is a very healthy vegetable (especially good for intestines). In ancient China, it is said that they had the burdock in place of medicine. Carrots are also good for the health so you can imagine how valuable it is. This is rather a grandmother's dish.

The name "Kimpira" comes from the very strong Samurai warrior who lived in the 12th century. He was so tough that they came to use his name for some goods such as Kimpira paste, Kimpira socks or Kimpira dolls. The burdock dish makes people so strong that ancient people named this just "Kimpira".

GADO GADO (MIXED SALAD)
(INDONESIAN STYLE)

Preparation time: 20 minutes

Serves 4

1 small white cabbage
2 carrots
8 oz (200 g) long green beans
8 oz (200 g) bean sprouts
1/2 a cucumber
3 tomatoes (cut into quarters)
1 broccoli (cut into florets)

SAUCE:

8 oz (200 g) peanuts (peeled) and ground
1 or 2 red fresh chillies (finely sliced)
2 tablespoons ketchup manis (Sweet Indonesian Soya Sauce)
A pinch of salt
1/2 teaspoon of chilli powder

METHOD:

1. Wash all vegetables. Cut cabbage into half and then finely slice. Peel and finely slice the carrots diagonally and then layer them together and slice again finely. Finely slice the long beans about 1 inch diagonally. Rinse the bean sprouts and drain. Cut broccoli into florets.

2. Blanch beans, broccoli and cabbage for 2 minutes and drain.

3. Finely slice the tomatoes and cucumber. Arrange vegetables on a plate by laying them individually.

4. Mix the sauce ingredients, that is chillies, sweet soya sauce and salt in a bowl with the ground peanuts. Pour it over the salad. Garnish with lime juice. Serve with rice.
   Or arrange vegetables on a large plate in sections and put a bowl of peanut sauce in the centre of the plate.

YUM YAI
(THE GREAT THAI SALAD)

Preparation time: 20 minutes

Serves 4

1 cucumber
5 lettuce leaves
1/2 cup mint leaves for garnishing
1/2 cup coriander leaves for garnishing
1 cup finely sliced boiled lean pork
1 cup finely sliced boiled prawns
1 cup dried black mushrooms
1 hard boiled egg
4 tablespoons fish soya sauce
4 tablespoons lime juice
1 tablespoon sugar

METHOD:

1. Peel and slice the cucumber. Wash and cut the lettuce into small pieces. Soak mushrooms in water until soft and drain and cut off the hard stems. Boil the mushrooms and finely slice.

2. Cut the hard boiled egg lengthways into 8 pieces. Mix the fish sauce, lime juice and sugar or the salad dressing. Put the vegetables, boiled lean pork and prawns in a bowl.

3. Pour in the dressing and toss well. Decorate the top with the egg segments, coriander and mint leaves.

PAKORAS
(VEGETABLE BHAJIS)

Cooking time: 25 minutes
Preparation time: 20 minutes

Serves 4

6 oz (115 g) gram flour (yellow)
1 potato (finely sliced)
1 aubergine (finely sliced) optional
4 oz (100 g) cauliflower (finely sliced)optional
2 to 3 fresh green chillies (finely sliced)
1/2 teaspoon red chilli powder
1/2 teaspoon garam masala
1/2 teaspoon cummin seeds

3/4 pinch of salt
Fresh coriander leaves (chopped)
8 tablespoons water to make batter
Oil for deep-frying

METHOD:

1. To make the batter, put the flour into a bowl and add water and mix with a fork until the batter is quite sticky, but not too runny. Add more water if necessary.

2. Wash all the vegetables and finely slice them. Once the vegetables has been prepared add them to the batter and mix well. Then add all the spices and coriander leaves.

3. Heat the oil in a deep pan and when it is very hot, add 1 dessertspoon of the vegetable mixture into the oil for about 1 to 2 minutes each side and turn over until brown in colour.

4. Repeat until all the batter is used up. This dish can be used as a snack or a starter dish.

NA TANG
(PARTY DIP)

Preparation time: 20 minutes

Serves 4

1 cup ground cooked pork or minced meat (cooked)
1/2 cup ground dried prawns
2 1/2 cups of coconut milk
1/2 cup lightly roasted peanuts
1/2 cup finely sliced shallots (peeled)
1 teaspoon salt
1/2 teaspoon sugar
A pinch of pepper
A few coriander leaves

METHOD:

1. Put the coconut milk into a small saucepan and bring to the boil. Reduce heat and simmer for a few minutes.

2. Add all the ingredients and stir well until cooked. Season with salt, pepper and sugar. Then add peanuts and mix well and remove from the heat. Before serving garnish with coriander leaves. This is a special dip for party time.

LON TAO CHEORN
(VEGETABLES WITH THAI SAVOURY DIP)

Cooking time: 10 minutes
Preparation time: 15 minutes

Serves 4

5 tablespoons soya bean paste (Tao Cheorn) brown colour
7 oz (200 g) small prawns
7 oz (200 g) minced pork
1 packet (60 g) dried coconut cream powder
1½ cups of water
4 dried chillies
3 tablespoons sliced red onions
5 tablespoons sugar
1 teaspoon salt
2 tablespoons tamarind juice
3 red whole chillies
½ a cucumber (finely sliced)
1 large carrot (cut into thin strips)
1 egg plant (aubergine) finely sliced
1 white cabbage (cut into 1 inch pieces)

METHOD:

1. Peel the prawns and chop them into pieces. Pound or blend the soya bean (Tao Cheorn). Pound or blend the dried chillies and the red onions together for 1 minute.

2. Mix the coconut with 1½ cups of water and heat in a small saucepan until it thickens. Then put the minced pork, prawns, blended soya bean, sliced chillies, red onions together into another saucepan and add the coconut milk gradually, stirring until well mixed. Cook for about 10 minutes.

3. Reduce the heat adding sugar, salt and tamarind juice. Then simmer for about 10 minutes, and add the whole red chillies.

4. Remove from heat and serve with cucumber, carrot, egg plant and cabbage.

TIPS:

Use 2 oz of Tamarind fruit soak in a small cup of water for about 10 minutes. Then drain the juice and discard the stones. Tamarind juice is use for making curry or fish dishes. It has a sweet and sour taste.

Most Thai recipes use Nam Pla fish soya sauce. If using this sauce, be very sparing with salt, as you can overdo it and end up with a too salty dish.

VEGETABLE STIR-FRY
(TAIWANESE STYLE)

Cooking time: 20 minutes
Preparation time: 10 minutes

1 leek
1 green and 1 red pepper
6 to 8 mushrooms
1 medium carrot
2 to 3 cloves of garlic (chopped)
1 tablespoon oyster sauce
1 dessertspoon cornflour mixed
   with 2 tablespoons water to a cream
2 tablespoons vegetable oil

METHOD:

1. Wash and cut leeks into 1 inch wide pieces. Wash and de-seed peppers and cut into strips and then into small squares. Wash and peel mushrooms and finely slice.

2. Heat the wok until hot, add oil then add garlic and stir-fry until light brown. Add all the vegetables and fry for 15 minutes on medium heat. Reduce heat a little and add oyster sauce and stir for a further minute.

3. Add the cornflour mixture and continue stirring for 2 minutes until vegetables are soft. Add more water if necessary so that sauce is not too thick.

TIPS:
This vegetarian dish can be eaten by itself or served with rice or noodles.

STIR FRIED PICKLED CABBAGE WITH PRAWNS

Cooking time: 18 minutes
Preparation time: 15 minutes

1 pickled Chinese cabbage
8 oz (225 g) fresh prawns or frozen prawns
3 cloves garlic (chopped)
2 tablespoons vegetable oil
2 to 3 tablespoons water

METHOD:

1. Rinse the pickled cabbage and cut into half an inch wide. Wash and peel prawns.

2. Heat the wok with oil until hot, add garlic and stir fry for 1 to 2 minutes until light brown.

3. Then add the prawns and stir fry for 3 to 5 minutes and add the pickled cabbage and stir again for 5 minutes. Add water and stir frequently for 10 minutes until prawns are cooked and the colour should be pink. Add more water if necessary, so that it is not to dry. Transfer into a dish and serve.

TIPS:

Pickled cabbage is sold in Chinese Supermarkets. It is better to use fresh prawns because the taste is much sweeter.

ODEN
(MIXED VEGETABLE)

Cooking time: 30 minutes
Preparation: 20 minutes

Serves 4

1 carton Tofu (white bean curd)
1 square piece Connyaku (square piece potato jelly)
or use 1 packet transparent Chinese noodles for substitute
4 hard boiled eggs
6 to 8 new potatoes
4 pieces of Hannpenn (fish-paste) made from fish
or substitute with 4 chipolata sausages
4 radishes (peeled)
1 packet of Dashi soup

SAUCE INGREDIENTS:

$1/2$ cup of miso
$3/4$ cup of sugar
2 tablespoons of water

METHOD:

1. Put sauce ingredients into a small saucepan and boil once and simmer for 10 minutes, stirring all the time. This is used as a dipping sauce. The sauce should be quite thick.

2. Place tofu on a plate and then press lightly so as to squeeze off the water. After 30 minutes, heat a frying pan with 1 tablespoon of oil and fry the tofu on both sides until brown for 5 minutes.

3. Cut the potato jelly (connyaku) into bite size pieces about 2 inches long.

4. Peel the eggs and remove the shells.

5. Boil the new potatoes until soft.

6. Peel and boil the radishes until soft. Cut into bite size pieces.

7. When all the ingredients have been cooked, transfer them onto a large saucepan with the dashi soup and add a teaspoon of salt and a tablespoon of soya sauce and boil for about 15 minutes. Serve with dipping sauce.

TIPS:
The longer you boil the vegetables, the better the taste. Oden food shop owners have been using the same dashi soup for a very long period, about half a century. Dashi soup packet is sold in Japanese or Chinese Supermarkets.
Chinese transparent noodles are used for making soup or stir fried dishes.

BRAISED PORK IN BROWN SAUCE
(TAIWAN STYLE)

Cooking time : 60 minutes
Preparation time : 10 minutes

Serves 2

1 lb (450 g) lean pork or pork spareribs
2 tablespoons vegetable oil
1 dessertspoon sugar
A 2 inch piece of ginger (finely sliced)
2 to 3 cloves garlic (chopped)
2 scallions (long onions) diagonally sliced
2 tablespoons white wine
1 to 2 teaspoons dark soya sauce

METHOD:

1. Wash and pat dry the pork and cut into 2 inch pieces.

2. Heat oil in wok until quite hot, add pork and stir fry for 3 minutes.

3. Then add the sugar, ginger, garlic, scallion, wine and soya sauce and stir fry for 2 minutes. Add more soya sauce if necessary.

4. Cook on low heat and simmer for 50 minutes until meat is tender.

PORK SPARERIBS WITH BALSAM PEARS
(TAIWAN STYLE)

Cooking time : 60 minutes
Preparation time : 10 minutes

Serves 2

2 pork spareribs
2 balsam pears or any pears
2 to 3 oz fresh or dried small fishes (optional)
1 dessertspoon black bean sauce
1 pint of water

METHOD:

1. Wash pork and pat dry, then cut into 1 inch pieces.

2. Peel and cut pears into small pieces.

3. Boil 1 pint of water in saucepan and during boiling drop in the pork, pears and dried or fresh fish. Boil on medium heat for 30 minutes.

4. During cooking add black bean sauce and stir. Simmer for 30 minutes until meat is tender.

TIPS:
If serving 4 persons then use 2 more spareribs.

PORK (ADOBO)
(PHILIPPINES STYLE)

Cooking time: 40 minutes
Preparation time: 10 minutes

Serves 4

1 lb (450 g) spare -ribs or belly pork (cut into 1 inch cubes)
5 to 6 cloves of garlic (peeled and crushed)
2 tablespoons vinegar (white or brown)
1 teaspoon whole black pepper (whole or crushed)
2 to 3 (fresh or dried) bay leaves
1 teaspoon fresh ginger (peeled and finely sliced)
3 tablespoons dark soya sauce
1 tablespoon fish sauce
1 dessertspoon sugar

METHOD:

1. Mix all the ingredients (except pork) in a bowl and add 1 dessertspoon sugar and salt.
    Taste it first before adding the fish sauce. Add more fish sauce if necessary.

2. Wash pork and marinate with the sauce for at least 1 hour or over night in the refrigerator.
    Cover with lid.

3. Put into a pyrex or tray and cover with lid and cook on Gas Mark 4 350° F/180° C.
    for about 30 to 40 minutes until meat is tender.

4. Serve with boiled rice.

SPARE RIBS KING

Cooking time: 20 to 25 minutes
Preparation time: 10 minutes

Serves 4

8 spare ribs
1$^1/_2$ tablespoons of Worcestershire sauce
2 teaspoons wine
1 teaspoon salt
1 teaspoon dark soya sauce
3 tablespoons water
4 tablespoons sugar
1 teaspoon sesame oil
1 tablespoon cornflour

METHOD:

1. Use a mallet to hammer the ribs a few times to flatten them. Then sliced the ribs into $^1/_2$ inch thick slices.

2. Marinate the spare ribs in a Pyrex dish with Worcestershire sauce, wine, sugar, dark soya sauce, sesame oil, and salt for 3 to 4 hours in a fridge. Cover with lid.

3. Heat wok with 1 tablespoon oil until hot and stir fry ribs for 20 to 25 minutes until meat is tender. Mix cornflour with 3 tablespoons water to make it creamy and pour over the meat.

FRIED PORK STEAKS
(MALAYAN STYLE)

Cooking time: 20 minutes
Preparing time: 10 minutes

Serves 4

4 pork chops
2 dessertspoons fine breadcrumbs
2 tomatoes (coarsely sliced)
1 dessertspoon thick soya sauce
   (mixed with $^1/_2$ cup of water)
2 large onions (coarsely sliced)
4 dessertspoons vegetable oil
A pinch of salt
A pinch of pepper

METHOD:

1. Heat oil in a large frying pan on medium heat. Add salt and pepper to the pork. Coat each piece lightly with breadcrumbs and fry the pieces, turning over when brown.

2. Reduce the heat a little, add soy sauce and cover the pan allowing pork to simmer until it is cooked. Push the pork to one side of the pan and fry the onions and tomatoes until they are a little soft. Serve with rice.

3. Add more soya sauce if necessary and water if more gravy is needed.

PORK AND CABBAGE DUMPLING
(TAIWANESE STYLE)

Cooking time: 30 minutes
Preparation time: 15 minutes

Serves 4

6 oz (175 g) pork finely sliced
1 small white cabbage (finely sliced)
1 medium onion (finely sliced)
A few spring onions (chopped)
2 tablespoons vegetable or peanut oil for frying
1 litre or 2 pints water
6 oz (175 g) plain flour
1 large egg
A pinch of salt
3 to 4 tablespoons milk or water

METHOD:

TO MAKE THE DOUGH:

1. Sift flour into a bowl and add the egg and whisk, adding milk a little at a time until it is very sticky. Sprinkle flour on the board and then knead the dough for 10 minutes.

2. First roll it into a long dough and then cut into several 2 inch pieces and roll each one into a small ball. Next flatten the pastry and fill it with 1 teaspoonful of meat ingredients and seal the edge with milk, by folding the pastry over to one side. Leave it on the plate and cover with a damp cloth until ready to use.

3. Heat the wok until quite hot, add the oil and onions and fry for 2 minutes until light brown, then add meat and stir for 5 minutes. Add cabbage and spring onions and continue frying for a further 10 minutes. Add salt and pepper to taste and set aside. Use this meat mixture for the fillings.

4. Boil 2 pints of water into a large saucepan and when it is boiling, drop the dumplings a few at a time until the dumplings float on the surface then they are ready to eat.

5. Serve dumplings with chilli sauce or soya sauce.

TOM YAM KUNG
(THAI HOT AND SOUR PRAWN SOUP)

Cooking time : 30 minutes
Preparation time : 15 minutes

Serves 4

1 lb (450 g) fresh prawns
2 to 3 sticks lemon grass (cut into 2 inch length) crushed
2 red chillies (sliced diagonally)
A few sprigs of coriander leaves (chopped)
1 dessertspoon lime or lemon juice
1 dessertspoon Tom Yam chilli paste
1 litre of water (2 pints)
Salt to taste
2 dessertspoons sugar

METHOD:

1. If fresh prawns are used, rinse and boil the prawns with shells in a large saucepan for 10 to 15 minutes. Add lemon grass, chillies and Tom Yam paste and stir. When the prawns turn pink in colour, they are cooked.

2. Drain the prawns and cool. Peel the prawns and set aside. Return the shells to the pan to continue cooking for a further 15 minutes. During cooking add coriander leaves, lemon juice, salt and sugar to taste.

3. Put soup through muslin or a strainer. Discard the rest of the ingredients. Return soup to the pan, add prawns and simmer for 5 minutes.

4. Taste soup to see if you need more salt or chilli paste. Serve with boiled rice on its own or as a starter dish.

TIPS:

This is a very hot and sour soup which is cooked to suit your taste depending how hot you like it. The prawns should be added in the last 5 minutes. Do not use too much chilli paste if you prefer it mild.

OYAKO DOMBURI
(JAPANESE CHICKEN RICE SOUP)

Cooking time: 35 minutes
Preparation time: 25 minutes

Serves 4

12 oz (350 g) chicken breast (seasoned)
6 medium eggs (1^1/$_2$ eggs each person)
A few spring onions (diagonally sliced or
^{1}/$_2$ an onion finely sliced)
2 cups of rice
1 packet of Dashi soup
1 tablespoon vegetable oil

METHOD:

1. Wash onion and slice. Finely slice the chicken breast into about ^{1}/$_2$ inch square. Use 2 cups of rice with 2 cups of water for boiling. It takes 25 minutes to cook.

2. Mix Dashi soup with 1 pint of water, 1 teaspoon of soya sauce, a pinch of salt, a pinch of Aji-no-moto, ^{1}/$_3$ teaspoon of sugar and boil for 5 minutes.

3. Heat a small frying pan with 1 dessertspoon of oil until hot, add the chicken breast and onion and stir for about 6 to 8 minutes. This should be enough for 4 servings.

4. Put $1/4$ of the soup which is prepared into a small saucepan and reheat, then add $1/4$ of the chicken breast. Then pour $1^1/_2$ beaten egg over the chicken. Put rice into individual bowls and serve with chicken and soup on top. Garnish with spring onions.

5. Prepare each bowl individually.

TIPS:

This dish is known as Mother and Child Bowl (Oyako Domburi)

SHARK'S FIN SOUP
(PENANG CHINESE STYLE)

Cooking time: 30 minutes
Preparation time: 15 minutes

Serves 4

5 oz (150 g) shark's fins
1 lb (450 g) crab or use a small tin crab
1 piece ham (35 g) cut into small pieces
1 lb (450 g) pork or beef (finely slices)
4 hard boiled egg (chopped)
2 teaspoons vegetable oil
1.1 litre of water
2 to 3 tablespoons cornflour
A pinch of Aji-no-moto
A pinch of salt
1 tablespoon light soya sauce
1 teaspoon white wine
6 eggs (beaten)

METHOD:

1. Wash and clean the shark's fins. Slice the meat. Chop the ham. Hard boil 4 eggs. Beat 6 eggs into a bowl and set aside.

2. First mix corn flour with 1.1 litre of water. Then heat a large saucepan with 2 teaspoons of oil and the cornflour with water. When it is boiling add 1 teaspoon wine, aji-no-moto and 1 tablespoon soya sauce.

2. Next add the shark's fins, meat, crabs, boiled eggs and boil for 30 minutes, finally add the beaten egg and stir for 2 minutes and switch off. Add salt to taste.

3. Serve with rice or can be used as a starter dish or main dish.

SUMASHI JIRU
(VEGETABLE SOUP)

Cooking time: 25 minutes
Preparation time: 15 minutes

Serves 4

1 packet Dashi soup
1/2 teaspoon salt
1 tablespoon soya sauce
4 cups of water
A pinch Aji-no-moto
Chinese green leaves or
Chinese white cabbage
1 carton Tofu (white bean curd)
6 oz (175 g) Chinese or Japanese mushrooms
8 oz (225 g) Japanese fish paste also known as "kamaboko"

METHOD:

1. Wash all the vegetables and cut into pieces of 1 inch wide. Cut green beans into 2 inch lengths. Cut tofu into 8 pieces.

2. Soak mushrooms in water for 20 minutes until soft and drain. Finely slice the mushrooms. The juice can be use for making the soup because it is very tasty.

3. Mix the packet of Dashi with 4 cups of water. Boil the soup for about 15 minutes with all the ingredients and then simmer for 10 minutes. Add the tofu in the last 5 minutes as it does not take long to cook.

TOMATO AND ONION SOUP WITH BEEF
(TAIWAN STYLE)

Cooking time : 60 minutes
Preparation time : 10 minutes

Serves 4

2 beef (sirloin)
2 tomatoes
2 sticks of celery
1 small onion
A few small potatoes
1 Chinese white cabbage
2 cloves of garlic (chopped)
2 pints of water
A pinch of salt
A pinch of black pepper

METHOD:

1. Wash and cut beef into 1 inch square pieces. Cut tomatoes into 1 inch pieces.

2. Wash and cut celery into small pieces. Finely slice the onions. Cut potatoes into small cubes.

3. Wash the cabbage. Do not cut cabbage, but tear into about 2 inch pieces.

4. Boil 2 pints of water in a deep medium saucepan. Then add all the ingredients with salt and black pepper to taste. Cook for 30 minutes and simmer for 30 minutes.

MISO SOUP
(JAPANESE SOUP)

Cooking time: 25 minutes
Preparation time: 20 minutes

Serves 4

1 packet of Dashi soup (mix with 4 cups of water)
2 spring onions (chopped)
4 oz (100 g) Chinese or Japanese mushrooms (sliced)
1/2 Chinese cabbage (cut into 1 inch length)
or any green vegetable you prefer
or 5 to 6 oz (150 g to 175 g) bean sprouts
2 teaspoons of miso paste
1 carton of Tofu (bean curd) cut into bite size pieces

METHOD:

1. Soak the mushrooms in water for 15 to 20 minutes until soft and drain. The mushroom juice can be use for making the soup. Wash all the vegetables and finely slice.

2. Boil the Dashi soup for about 15 to 20 minutes with all the vegetables in a medium saucepan. After boiling reduce the heat.

3. Then add two teaspoons of miso paste. Put the miso paste through a metal strainer and stir it through into the saucepan. Do not boil the miso.

3. After cooking for 20 minutes add Tofu (bean curd) pieces and cook for 3 to 4 minutes. Then remove the saucepan off the heat.

TIPS:

Miso soup is served for breakfast in a Japanese home. Dashi soup and miso paste are sold in dried packets in Japanese supermarkets or Chinese supermarkets. If Dashi soup is not available, the juice of Chinese mushrooms can be use to make the soup.

METHOD:

1. Finely slice the Chinese mushrooms. Put a round bowl on the top part of the melon and draw a circle. Then use a sharp knife to cut the top off and trim it neatly round the edge in a zig zag pattern.

2. Scoop out all the melon into 10 to 12 balls and save for later. Discard the seeds. Make sure the melon is empty.

3. Heat a saucepan with the chicken stock and boil for 15 minutes. Add the chicken and stir, then add mushrooms and stir.

4. Add the cuttle fish and dates to the stock. Finally add the melon balls and Aji-no-moto, Chinese wine, salt and pepper to taste and boil for a further 15 minutes until chicken is tender.

5. Arrange the water melon in a big bowl. Transfer the hot soup into the water melon and serve hot as a starter dish.

OYSTER SOUP

Cooking time: 20 minutes
Preparation: 20 minutes

Serves 4

10 oz (300 g) fresh oysters
5 cups of Dashi soup
1 tablespoon light soya sauce
$3/4$ teaspoon salt
1 tablespoon Japanese Wine (Sake)
A pinch of Aji-no-moto
A few spring onions
6 Chinese mushrooms
1 tablespoon vegetable oil

METHOD:

1. Soak mushrooms in water until soft and squeeze. Prepare the Dashi soup first. Wash the vegetables and finely slice diagonally. Finely slice the mushrooms.

2. Wash the oysters well. Take meat out of shells by using a sharp knife. Heat a medium saucepan with 1 tablespoon of vegetable oil and fry the oysters for 5 minutes.

3. Boil the soup once and add the mushrooms, vegetables, oysters and add salt to taste.

TIPS:
This soup can be eaten in the morning or afternoon.
Mushroom juice can be use for making the soup as it is very tasty. So you can mix it with the Dashi soup to make up to 5 cups. Dashi soup is sold dried in packets in Japanese or Chinese Supermarkets.

SUSHI RICE

Cooking time: 40 minutes
Preparation time: 25 minutes

Serves 4

Ingredients for Sushi rice:

3 cups of Japanese rice or Californian rice
3 cups of water + 3 tablespoons of Japanese Wine (Sake)
A pinch of salt
$1/10$ cup of rice vinegar (60 ml)
1 tablespoon of sugar
A piece of kelp for aroma (4 inch length)
if not available use a pinch of Aji-no-moto

INGREDIENTS TO BE MIX WITH THE RICE

4 oz Chinese mushrooms (100 g)
1 large carrot
4 oz (100 g) Connyaku (jelly made from potato)
or use parsnips
1 dessertspoon sugar
1 tablespoon Japanese Wine (Sake)

METHOD:

1. Rinse the rice bran by squeezing and rubbing rice until the milky water becomes clear. Repeat 3 times and cover with lid. Add water to the washed rice with a piece of "kelp" which is a green dried seaweed for aroma. Then leave the rice for 30 minutes before boiling.

2. Boil the rice for about 25 minutes until soft and fluffy. Then let the rice settled for about 10 minutes before use. Boil the vinegar, sugar, Sake and salt in a small saucepan for about 10 minutes, switch off and cool. When the rice is still hot, pour the vinegar over the rice. Fan the rice for 7 to 8 minutes, use a wooden spatula to separate the rice vertically.

3. Soak the Chinese mushrooms in water until soft and drain. Finely slice the carrot diagonally and then stack them on top of each other and finely slice again. Cut the Connyaku (jelly) into small cubes or substitute for transparent white Chinese noodles.

4. Boil all the vegetables in a medium saucepan with $2/3$ juice of the mushrooms, one tablespoon Sake, 1 teaspoon soya sauce, 1 dessertspoon sugar and a pinch of salt. Boil for 15 to 20 minutes until vegetables are soft and the juice is reduced. Then taste it to see if more soya sauce is needed. Switch off and cool down the vegetables.

5. Now mix all the vegetables with the sushi rice (using a wooden spoon) which was prepared earlier on and serve. This dish tastes really delicious.

Cooking time: 25 minutes
Preparation time: 15 minutes

Serves 4 to 6

3 cups of Japanese rice or Californian rice
3 cups of water + 3 tablespoons of Sake
$^1/_{10}$ cup of rice vinegar (60 ml)
1 tablespoon sugar
A pinch of salt
1 piece of kelp for aroma (4 inch length) green dried seaweed
or use a pinch of Aji-no-moto
4 to 6 pieces of seaweed 7 x 7 inch square

METHOD:

1. Rinse the rice bran by squeezing and rubbing rice until the milky water becomes clear. Repeat 3 times and cover with lid. Add water to the washed rice with a piece of "kelp" which is used for aroma. Then leave the rice for 30 minutes before boiling.

2. Boil the rice for about 25 minutes until soft and fluffy. Then let the rice settle for about 10 minutes before use. Boil the rice vinegar, sugar, Sake and salt in small saucepan for 10 minutes and switch off and cool.

3. When the rice is settled, transfer it into a large dish and then pour the vinegar mixture over the rice. Then fan the rice quickly about for 7 to 8 minutes while making vertical lines across the rice by using a wooden spatula.

HOW TO ROLL THE SUSHI

STEP 1. Lay out a bamboo mat 9 $^1/_2$ x 9 $^1/_2$ inch square and lay a piece of black seaweed 7 x 7 inch square on top of the mat. Sprinkle a small amount of rice vinegar over the seaweed.

STEP 2. Leave half an inch space at the bottom of the seaweed and then put 2 dessert spoons of rice onto the seaweed and spread thinly to the top leaving half an inch space at the top.

STEP 3. Place 1 long strip of green and red pepper onto the seaweed from left to right and also 1 long strip of tuna or salmon. Wet both hands with the rice vinegar before rolling so that your hands do not stick to the rice.

STEP 4. Use the bamboo mat to help roll the sushi and gradually pull the mat towards yourself and continue rolling the sushi, leaving half an inch at the top for sealing. (Do not roll the sushi too tight as it may crack.) Once you've reached the top, wet the seaweed with a little vinegar to seal and roll to the end.

Then leave the sushi standing for at least 30 minutes to settle before cutting. To cut the sushi, first wet a sharp knife and slice into pieces about 1$^1/_2$ inches wide and serve on a tray.

STEP 1

STEP 2

1 carton To-Fu (Soya Bean Curd) white colour
1 to 2 tablespoons sugar
1 to 2 tablespoons light soya sauce
1 tablespoon vegetable oil or use beef fat

METHOD:

1. Slice beef into $1/2$ an inch wide. Wash vegetables and slice. Soak mushrooms in water until soft and drain.

2. Use a large griddle or a large heavy frying pan, heat it with oil until hot, grill the meat for 8 to 10 minutes then add soya sauce and sugar and stir, turning the meat over several times.

3. Add the vegetables and sugar, then soya sauce and Connyaku and stir frequently for 5 minutes.

4. Cut To-Fu into 8 pieces and add to the beef and vegetables. Continue stirring until meat is cooked. Taste to see if you need more soya sauce or sugar.

5. Crack 4 eggs, one into each individual bowl for dipping. Sukiyaki is to be dipped and stirred in these raw eggs for each guest.

TIPS:
This meal is cooked in small quantities at a time in the middle of the table. This is a Japanese way of entertaining their guests when they enjoy their conversations. It should be serve hot.
If Connyaku is not available, you can substitute for transparent Chinese noodles.

CHAWANMUSHI
(STEAMED MEAT AND VEGETABLES)

Cooking time: 15 minutes
Preparation time: 15 minutes

Serves 4

1 medium carrot (finely sliced)
4 mushrooms (finely sliced)
4 oz (100 g) cooked prawns (peeled)
2 slices of bacon (finely sliced)
or 4 oz (100 g) chicken breast (finely sliced)
4 broccoli florets or 1 oz (25 g) of peas
1 packet of Dashi soup (mix with 3 small cups of water)
1 medium egg
A pinch of Aji-no-moto
$1/2$ teaspoon of sugar
1 teaspoon light soya sauce

METHOD:

1. Prepare 4 cups ready. Sprinkle salt on prawns. If using chicken, dip chicken in light soya sauce and half cook the chicken. Carrots and broccoli should be half cooked for about 2 minutes. Mushrooms should be half cooked with a little sugar and soya sauce.

2. Put all the ingredients evenly into 4 cups. Put 1 egg with 3 cups of Dashi soup and $1/2$ teaspoon of sugar, a pinch of Aji-no-moto into a bowl and whisk it together and then pour evenly into each cup.

3. Boil enough water in the saucepan or wok until it reaches boiling point. Then cover the cups with lids and steam for about 7 minutes.

4. After 7 minutes, test it by removing the lids and use a skewer to prick the meat to see if it is cooked. The vegetables should be soft. If it is cooked the ingredients should not be sticky and should not move.

This is served as a starter dish.

LAW BAK (NGOR HIANG) (PENANG SPRING ROLLS)

Cooking time: 20 minutes
Preparing time: 10 minutes

Serves 10 to 12

2 lb (1 kilo) lean pork with a little fat
2 eggs
3 tablespoons sugar
1 heaped teaspoon five-spice powder
A sprinkle of soya sauce
1 teaspoon tapioca flour or use (corn flour)
2 big square pieces bean curd sheets for wrapping

METHOD:

1. Cut pork into 2 to 3 cm long strips and 1 cm thick slices. Put pork strips into a mixing bowl.

2. Crack the eggs into the bowl and mix well with the pork. Add sugar, soya sauce and tapioca flour (mix with a little water to a cream). It should not be watery.

3. Cut bean curd sheets into 3" x 4" pieces. Put 4 to 5 strips of pork on one end of the sheet, making sure there is an equal amount of lean meat.

4. Fold both ends in and roll the sheet towards the end and seal with milk. Deep-fry the spring rolls until golden brown. Then slice into 1 inch pieces. Serve with cucumber slices.

TO MAKE CHILLI SAUCE:

5 oz (150 g) chillies (blend finely)

Put blended chillies into a small saucepan, add 1 cup of water, sugar and vinegar to taste and boil until sauce is thick. Sprinkle with roasted sesame seeds just before serving. This sauce is use for dipping.

MURTABAK (INDIAN PANCAKE) (PENANG STYLE)

Cooking time: 30 minutes
Preparation time: 40 to 50 minutes

Serves 4

2 lb (1 kilo) Murtabak Flour (wheat flour)
1 small tin condensed milk
A pinch of salt
5 large eggs
1 glass water
1 dessertspoon sugar

METHOD:

1. Put flour into a large bowl with milk, eggs, salt, sugar and mix together with a wooden spoon. Then add water and mix again for 5 minutes. Knead the dough for 10 to 15 minutes and then cover with a damp cloth for 30 minutes.

2. When the dough has risen, roll them into small golf balls size. Once all the dough has been rolled up, flatten each ball by using both hands.

3. Next step is to oil the table top and place each ball on the table and flatten it until you get the size of an 8 inch pancake.

FILLINGS:

1 packet of masala powder
2 eggs
4 oz (100 g) mixed vegetables
1 large onion (finely sliced)
2 Chicken breasts (finely sliced)
or 1 tin of Tuna (drained)

1. Heat a medium saucepan with oil until hot add the onions and stir fry for 2 minutes. Then add the chicken and stir for 10 to 15 minutes until chicken is tender.

2. Add the vegetables and stir again, then add the masala powder and mix together with 2 tablespoons water and stir fry for 5 to 10 minutes and switch off.

3. Oil the grid or frying pan. Put each pancake onto a grid. Put 2 tablespoons of fillings into the centre of the pancake.

4. Fold edges inwards and cover with another thin piece of pancake. Leave for 2 to 3 minutes and turn over for 2 to 3 minutes until brown. Serve with curry sauce.

BANANA FRITTERS
(MALAYAN STYLE)

Cooking time : 15 minutes
Preparation time : 10 minutes

Serves 4

4 bananas
4 oz (100 g) plain flour
1 large egg
A pinch of salt
2 to 3 tablespoons milk
1 tin small golden syrup
1 litre oil for deep-frying

TO MAKE BATTER :

1. Sift flour in a bowl 3 times, then crack an egg into the centre and mix on speed 2 for 2 minutes. Add a little milk at a time until batter is quite sticky, but not too thick. Add salt to taste.

2. Peel bananas and then cut into halves lengthways. Put 2 bananas at a time into the batter and dip in then turn over once until well coated.

3. Heat oil in wok until very hot, drop in the bananas 2 or 3 at a time until golden brown and turn over once. Remove the bananas and put onto paper towel to absorb the oil. Repeat until all bananas are use up.

4. Heat golden syrup in a small saucepan until runny and pour over the bananas.

HONEY DEW MELON WITH SAGO

Cooking time: 25 minutes
Preparation time: 15 minutes

Serves 4

3 lb (1 kilo) Honey Dew Melon
1¼ oz (30 g) sago
150 ml Vanilla Ice Cream
⅛ teaspoon salt

METHOD:

1. Wash sago, soak in water for 10 minutes. Put a medium bowl on the top part of the melon and draw a circle. Use a sharp knife and cut the top off. Trim all round the edge of the melon in a zig zag pattern.

2. Scoop out the melon flesh and discard the seeds. Put the melon flesh into the blender with salt and blend for 1 to 2 minutes and switch off.

3. Boil sago for 20 to 25 minutes until soft and double in size. Then drain sago under running cold water.

4. Fill the hollow melon with the melon flesh and sago and stir with a spoon. Then scoop the vanilla ice cream on top of the melon and serve. Decorate with little umbrellas and cherries.

TIPS:
This is a mouth watering dessert.

EGG AND TOMATO JAFFLE
(BALI STYLE)

Cooking time: 10 minutes
Preparation time: 8 minutes

Serves 1

1 egg
1 tomato(sliced)
2 slices white bread
2 tablespoons vegetable or peanut oil
2 oz (50 g) butter or margarine

METHOD:

1. Heat the frying pan with oil and fry the egg. Butter the bread. Transfer the eggs onto a piece of bread with tomatoes and then cover with another piece of bread.

2. Sandwich them together and put it into a toaster maker for 2 to 3 minutes until light brown. Serve with tropical fruits.

If you are making this dish for 4 persons add 3 more of everything. So two slices of bread for each person.

This is what I have for my breakfast in Kuta, Bali. I also get a bowl of fruits and tea.

KHAI YAD SAI
(STUFFED THAI OMELETTE)

Cooking time: 20 minutes
Preparing time: 5 minutes

Serves 4

4 eggs
3 tablespoons fish soya sauce
2 onions (peeled and finely chopped)
4 oz (100 g) minced pork or beef
2 large tomatoes (finely chopped)
1 cup sweet peas (cleaned and shelled)
2 tablespoons tomato sauce
A pinch of pepper
2 tablespoons vegetable oil

METHOD:

1. First prepare the stuffing. Heat the wok with oil when hot add the onion and pork and stir-fry until golden brown, then add tomato sauce, chopped tomatoes, sweet peas, fish sauce and pepper to taste.

2. Stir-fry for about 5 minutes and then remove from heat.

3. To make the omelette, beat the eggs in a bowl and add the remaining fish sauce. Heat 1 tablespoon of oil in a frying pan and pour in enough of the beaten egg to cover the pan to make one omelette.

4. When the mixture starts to set, add a generous helping of the stuffing and fold the omelette over to one side. Remove from the heat and repeat the process until all is used up. Serve hot.

OMURAISU
(OMELETTE RICE)

Cooking time: 45 minutes
Preparation time: 15 minutes

Serves 4

2 cups of Japanese rice
$2^1/_4$ cups of water
1 medium onion (finely sliced into strips)
4 oz (100 g) chicken breast (finely sliced into strips)
$3^1/_2$ (80 g) canned peas
4 teaspoons vegetable oil
4 large eggs
A pinch of salt
1 teaspoon sugar
A pinch of Aji-no-moto
A teaspoon of cornflour
$1^1/_2$ cups tomato ketchup

METHOD:

1. Wash the rice several times until the water is clear and leave it for at least 15 minutes. Cook rice until soft and fluffy for 25 minutes. Let it settle for 10 minutes before use.

2. Heat the wok with 1 tablespoon of oil until quite hot, add the onions and cook until light brown and stir for 2 minutes, then add the chicken, peas and stir for 10 minutes until chicken is tender.

3.   Add the cooked rice to the chicken with 1 cup of tomato ketchup and continue stirring until well mixed and turn off heat. This should be for enough 4 servings.

4.   Next crack all the eggs in a bowl with salt, sugar and Aji-no-moto. Mix the cornflour with 1 teaspoon of water to a cream and add to the eggs and stir.

5.   Heat a frying pan with a teaspoon of oil until hot, add a quarter of the prepared egg mixture and spread round onto the pan thinly and fry for 2 to 3 minutes until light brown. Repeat this 4 times until you get 4 omelettes.

6.   Put the prepared rice, chicken and peas onto the omelette and then fold the omelette over and seal. Pour tomato ketchup over the omelette rice in the centre and serve. Repeat this 4 times.

KOAY KOH SWEE
(CHINESE COCOA RICE CAKE)

Cooking time: 20 minutes
Preparation time: 10 minutes

1 teaspoon cocoa powder
1 teaspoon cornflour
5$^{1}/_{2}$ oz (150 g) granulated sugar
1$^{1}/_{5}$ pint (600 ml) water
7 oz (200 g) rice flour

METHOD:

1.   Boil water in a large saucepan with sugar, for about 10 minutes until sugar is dissolved. Then pour the sugar syrup into another saucepan with cornflour and cocoa mixture and stir well.

2.   Then transfer this cocoa mixture into small cups or moulds and steam for 5 minutes covered with lid. Leave to cool for 10 minutes.

3.   Remove the cake from the mould by turning it upside down, using a knife to go round the edge of the mould. Decorate the cake with freshly shredded coconut.

KOAY TAH LAM
(STEAMED PANDAN CAKE WITH COCONUT)

Cooking Time: 45 minutes
Preparation Time: 10 minutes

1 lb (450 g) sugar
6 oz (175 g) rice flour
2 oz (50 g) green bean flour or known as "Mung Beans".
6 oz (175 g) Pandan leaves or substitute this with a few drops of green food colouring
1 teaspoon Lye water

COCONUT TOPPING:

12 fluid oz coconut milk (375 ml)
8 fluid oz water (200 ml)
1 teaspoon salt
2 oz (50 g) rice flour
2 oz (50 g) tapioca flour
Mix all these ingredients together and use it for filling the top layer of the cake.

MANGO DELIGHT
(PENANG STYLE)

Preparation time : 15 to 20 minutes

Serves 4

4 mangoes
4 oz (100 g) pistachio nuts (chopped)
11 oz (300 g) Bar plain dark chocolate
10 fl oz (284 ml) double cream
4 cherries
Angelica (green colour)

METHOD:

1. Peel mangoes and cut into small cubes and set aside.

2. Break chocolate into small pieces and put into a bowl. Place the bowl on top of a saucepan with hot but not boiling water until chocolate dissolves. Make sure water does not enter the bowl.

3. Whisk cream in bowl until fluffy and mix with the chocolate sauce.

4. Prepare 4 cocktail glasses ready. Put a layer of mango into each glass and then chocolate cream on top and repeat once more.

5. Sprinkle with pistachio nuts and then put a small blob of cream in the centre and place a cherry on top and place 1 angelica leaf on each side of the cherry.

TIPS:
Cut the angelica into 2 small pieces of leaf shapes for decoration.

MALAYAN FRUIT COCKTAIL

Cooking time : 15 minutes
Preparation time: 20 minutes

Serves 4

1 star fruit
1 tin lychee
1 mango
1 small ripe papaya
1 small packet strawberry jelly
8 oz (225 g) packet coconut cream
1 dessertspoon sugar
1 teaspoon rum or brandy
2 to 3 drops of food red colouring

METHOD:

1. Peel mango and cut into small pieces. Wash star fruit and cut into small pieces. Peel papaya and cut into halves, then scoop out all the black seeds and discard them. Cut papaya into small cubes. Drain the lychees.

2. Put jelly into a bowl. Then boil water and pour 3/4 pint of water over the jelly and stir with a fork until jelly dissolves. When the jelly is cool, put it in the refrigerator to set. This can be prepared the night before. Then scoop the jelly into small balls.

3. Prepare 4 cocktail glasses and fill with fruits and jelly.

4. Melt the coconut cream in a small saucepan on low heat with 1 dessertspoon of sugar, add 1 teaspoon of rum and stir continuously until cream and sugar is dissolved. Cool first, then pour cream over the fruit cocktail.

PAPAYA DRINKS

Preparation time: 10 minutes

Serves 2

1 medium papaya
$1\frac{1}{2}$ cups of crushed ice
2 dessertspoons sugar

METHOD:

1. Peel papaya and cut into half. Scoop out all the black seeds and discard. Cut papaya into medium pieces and put them into the electric blender and blend for 2 minutes.

2. Next transfer the papaya juice with the sugar syrup into tall glasses. Fill it with crushed ice and serve. Wet the rim of the glass and sprinkle sugar on it. Decorate with a little umbrella and two cherries.

TIPS:
Sugar syrup can be used instead of granulated sugar. Boil the sugar with $\frac{1}{2}$ a cup of water in a small pan until sugar dissolves. Cool it and use for making drinks.

PINEAPPLE DRINKS

Preparation time: 10 minutes

Serves 2

1 pineapple
2 dessertspoons sugar
$1\frac{1}{2}$ cups of crushed ice

METHOD:

1. Cut skins of pineapple by using a sharp knife. Then cut pineapple into 4 quarters. Cut off the hard bit in the middle and then slice the pineapples into small pieces.

2. Put pineapple into the blender and blend for 2 to 3 minutes. Transfer pineapple juice into tall glasses with the sugar syrup and fill it with crushed ice. Wet the rim of the glass and sprinkle sugar on it. Decorate it with a little umbrella and two cherries.

TIPS:
Sugar syrup can be used instead of granulated sugar. Boil the sugar with $\frac{1}{2}$ cup of water and until sugar dissolves. Cool it and use it for making drinks.

CONVERSION TABLES

WEIGHTS

Ounze (oz)	Pounds (lb)	Grams (gms)
0.5		14
1		28
1.5		43
2		57
3		85
4.25		113
5		142
6		170
7		198
8.5		227
9		255
10		283
11		312
12.75		240
16	1 lb	453
	2 lb	907
	3 lb	1360

VOLUME

Fluid Oz	Pints	M/Litres	Litres
1		28	
2		57	
3		85	
5	0.25	142	
10	0.5	284	
15	0.75	426	
20	1	568	
	1.25	710	
	1.5	852	
	1.75	994	
	1.76	1000	1
	2		1.14
	2.5		1.42
	3		1.71
	4		2.28
	8		4.55

MEASUREMENTS

Inches		Cms
0.25		0.6
0.5		1.3
1		2.5
2		5.1
3		7.6
4		10.2
5		12.7
6		15.2
7		17.8
8		20.3
9		22.9
10		25.4
11		27.9
12		30.5

OVEN TEMPERATURES

		°F	°C
MK1		275	140
MK2		300	150
MK3		325	160
MK4		350	180
MK5		375	190
MK6		400	200
MK7		425	220
MK8		450	230
MK9		475	240

NB: Tablespoons and teaspoons are measured level

From left to right:

1) Kicap Manis
2) Sesame Oil
3) Fish Sauce
4) Dark Soya Sauce
5) Light Soya Sauce
6) Chilli Sauce

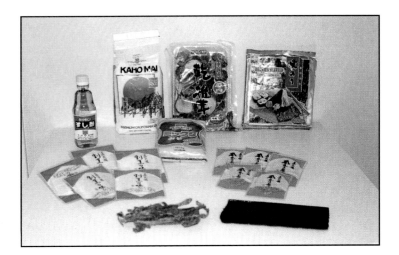

From left to right:

1) Japanese Rice Vinegar
2) Japanese Rice
3) Dried Mushroom
4) Seaweed

Middle:
Miso Soup (in packet)

Bottom Row:
From left to right:

1) Dashi Soup (in brown & orange packet)
2) Dried Kelp (seaweed)
3) Black Seaweed

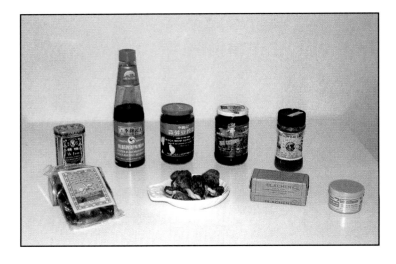

From left to right:

1) Aji-no-moto
2) Oyster Sauce
3) Black Bean Sauce
4) Brown Bean Sauce
5) Kimchu Chilli Sauce

Bottom Row:
From left to right:

1) Tamarind Fruit
2) Dried Mushroom

-3 & 4 are Prawn Paste (Blachan)

EQUIPMENT

A WOK

A wok is a Chinese frying pan used daily in every household or kitchen. It is round and deep, the diameter is 14 to 16 inch across. It is made from aluminium or heavy cast iron. But the modern day non-stick wok is very useful.

Before using a brand new wok, boil 2 pints of water for about 15 minutes then throw the water away. Then heat the wok with 2 tablespoons oil until hot, stir it several times. Throw the oil away. Rinse it with hot boiling water each time before use. Never scrub a wok. It will cook better each time it is used.

A wok is used for frying and steaming. Heat gets all the way round the wok so it will not take long to cook the food. Steaming is done by filling it with 2 pints of water and placing a wire tray inside the wok. You place the meat or fish on a metal plate and place it on the wire tray. Cover it with the lid for 10 minutes or more depending on cooking time.

Nowadays there is a modern type of wok which is electric. You cook in it in just the same way as the other type.

BAMBOO STEAMER

Bamboo steaming is an old fashioned method, but still used daily in restaurants. They come in different sizes and in three or even four layers with a lid. Large ones are used in restaurants, small ones are used in households.

Fill wok with enough water for steaming, keep checking to make sure that the water does not dry up, keep adding water if necessary. Always cover with a lid when steaming so that the food cooks quicker. With this method of cooking all the flavour is sealed in the food.

PESTLE AND MORTAR OR STONE POUNDER

A stone pounder is used throughout Malaysia. Every household has one. It is a round vessel made of stone about 6 inches in diameter with a deep hole in the middle. Spices are put into the stone pounder and pounded with the stone handle in order to make a smooth paste. Nowadays electric blenders can be used instead, as a modern alternative.

ELECTRIC RICE COOKER

It is advisable to use an electric rice cooker which is accurate with it's automatic timer and guarantees that the rice will not burn.

TECHNIQUES

MEAT

Meat like pork, beef or chicken can be cut into 1 inch cubes but mostly it is cut into thin strips about half an inch wide. Thin strips of meat will take less time to cook. Chicken meat is sometimes boned, however, Chinese believe that it tastes better if it's not. Chicken is usually chopped into bite size pieces for cooking.

STIR - FRYING

Stir frying is done in a wok for it's quickness. Meat and vegetables are sliced very thin so that it does not take too long to cook. The method is to keep stirring all the time until meat and vegetables are cooked.

STEAMING

Steaming is another method of cooking. It can be done in the wok or a bamboo steamer. Once the food is cooked the flavour is sealed. Fill the steamer or wok with 1 or 2 pints of water, when it boils place a wire tray across the wok. Put the meat or fish to be steamed onto a metal plate and put onto a tray. Cover with lid.

TO DE-VEIN PRAWNS

Prawns have shells on them. Normally these are peeled off with the heads, tails and all the legs. When cooking curry the heads and tails are usually left on because it gives the curry a sweeter flavour. To de-vein a prawn you slit it right up the middle into two halves. Take the grey coloured vein out, then cut the head and tail off before cooking.

VEGETABLES

Different types of vegetables are cut up in different ways. For long green beans you cut it into 2 inch lengths. Carrots are sliced cross ways very thinly, piled up on top of each other and then sliced thin again, it should look like it has been shredded. Cucumbers can be sliced across in 1/2 inch thickness. For Chinese green leaves you cut it into 2 inch lengths. Chinese white cabbage is cut into 1 inch lengths. The whole idea is that the thinly sliced vegetables will not take too long to cook.

CHILLIE PASTE

Chillie paste is made from dried chillies, lemon-grass, yellow ginger, shallots (small onions), blachan (prawn-paste) and garlic. Pound or blend all spices together into a smooth paste. It is now ready for use and will keep in a refrigerator for 1 to 2 weeks.

TECHNIQUES

CHILLIE SAUCE

Chillie sauce is made from fresh red chillies which are put into an electric blender with a little water. Blend into a smooth paste. Keep it handy in the fridge.

COCONUT MILK

Coconuts are normally used fresh. Old coconut kernels (the white flesh inside) that have gone hard can be cut into 4 or 5 pieces and put into a grinder. When it comes out it looks soft and shredded. Mix with a few spoons of water and put into a muslin and squeeze into a bowl. A thick milk comes out. You can repeat this 3 or 4 times with some more water, each time squeezing the milk into a bowl. Once you have got about one cup full of the thick milk, you can then add water to make the amount you need. The coconut can be discarded or you can fry it with some sugar and use it as candy.

DEEP-FRYING

Deep frying can be done in a wok if enough cooking oil is used. Put the meat or fish into the oil when it is hot enough and the temperature is right. The oil can be used again if put into a container when cool and covered with a lid.

GRILLING

Grilling is done over a charcoal fire or a small stove. Fire wood can also be used instead of charcoal. Meat is put onto long skewers across the fire, keep turning them over several times until the meat is roasted. A modern alternative is to use a gas or electric grill. A barbecue stove is another method of grilling.

MARINATING

The meat is cut into strips or 1 inch cubes. It is then put into a casserole dish with spice. Rub spices all over the meat and cover with a lid. Leave it in the refrigerator overnight, the meat will be well flavoured with the spice before being used for cooking. The meat should be left to marinate for a least 3 hours. When the meat has been cooked it will have a lovely aroma and flavour to it.

GLOSSARY

Abalone Fish	Roundish shape fish.
Aji-no-moto	To flavour any soup or vegetable dish.
Aubergine	Long, purple coloured vegetable.
Bamboo shoots	Creamy white look, crispy. Can be obtained in tins.
Beancurds	Made from soya beans, light creamy colour. Is square shaped can be bought fresh in cartons.
Bean (brown)	Brownish colour, creamy. Sold in jars, salted flavour.
Bean (white)	Use for puddings and drinks. Round beige colour.
Bean (black)	Salted spicy fermented soya beans.
Beans (long)	Green bean about 12" long. Very crispy when cooked.
Beansprouts	White slim shiny, crispy bean. Use for salad or stir-fry.
Blachan Paste	Made from prawns. Greyish in colour, strong smell, nice flavour.
Bunga Kelantan	A pink curry flower use especially for sweet and sour fish curry. Gives a nice aroma and flavour.
Candle nuts	A waxy looking nuts known as "kemiri" in Indonesia. Also known as "Buah Keras" in Malay language. It gives a creamy texture to thicken sauce.
Cardamon Pods	Brown pods have the most aromatic black seeds. Green ones have less aroma.
Cashew nuts	Shaped like a kidney and when roasted tastes very nice. Can be use for cooking.
Chillies	There are fresh red and green chillies. Red ones are hotter.
Chillies (green)	Small short chillies are very hot. Long ones are not so hot.
Chillies (dried)	Need to soak in water until soft and drain before use. Quite hot.
Chillie Powder	Dried chillies are ground into powder. Use to flavour curry dish.
Chillie Paste	Made from 5 different spices ground or blend together.

Chinese cabbage	White, pale green cabbage. Can use for salad.
Chinese Jelly	White transparent, looks like white straw. To make jelly, boil in 1 pint of water. Add colouring and sugar to taste.
Chinese leaf	Green in colour. Use for stir-fry.
Cinnamon stick	Brown coloured stick about 3" long. Use for flavouring curries.
Coriander	Round shaped seed, beige colour, use for garnish curry dish.
Coriander leaf	Fresh green leaves chopped, use for garnish curry dish.
Coconut milk	Milk from coconut flesh, ground.
Cummin seeds	Beige colour, oval shaped, whole or ground use for flavouring curry dish.
Dashi soup	Dashi soup is made from fish in Japan.
Enoki mushrooms	Thin white long Japanese mushrooms grows in bunches.
Fennel seeds	Taste like aniseed.
Five spice	Chinese ground spice made from star-anise, fennel, cloves, cinnamon and Sichuan peppercorns.
Galangal	Part of the ginger family, known as "Lengkuas" in Malay or Laos. Can be bought fresh or dried in packets. Soak in water until soft drain, before use.
Garam Masala	Five spices made from ground coriander, cinnamon stick, cumin seeds, cardamon pods and cloves.
Garlic	Grows in clusters. Use to garnish food.
Ghee	Pure white butter use for Indian curry dish.
Ginger (white)	Fresh ginger root. It has a sharp taste.
Ginger (yellow)	Yellow in colour. Also known as "Turmeric" in Indian. Also use for colouring the food and for flavouring.
Krupuk	Wafer, when fried they are crispy, use as a snack or side dish.
Ladies fingers	Green finger-shaped vegetable. Can be fried or cooked in curry.
Lemon grass	Known as "Serai" in Malay language. Use for curry dishes.

Lime juice	Green coloured fruit. Sour taste, very sharp. Use for garnish.
Lychees	White creamy soft fruit, outer skin is brown. Easy to peel. Available fresh from Chinese Supermarkets or tin.
Mint leaves	Green fresh mint leaves use in for garnish, or use as sauce.
Mushrooms	Dried Chinese mushrooms. Soak in water until soft before use.
Noodles	Made from flour and egg. Yellow in colour. Sold fresh or dried.
Oils	Three types of oils use for cooking. Peanut, coconut and vegetable oil.
Okras	Also known as "Ladies fingers" in Malaysia. Green finger shaped.
Oyster sauce	Made from oyster. Very tasty, thick brown sauce to flavour meat.
Pandan leaves	Leaves are used for aroma as well as for colouring food.
Peanuts	Salted peanuts sold in packets, or fresh. Grows in bunches.
Peppers	Fresh green or red peppers. Red peppers are sweet and green are spicy. Can be use raw for salad.
Prawns	Fresh prawns are available from markets. While cooked prawns are available in supermarkets. Tin prawns are in brine.
Prawns (dried)	Soak in water until soft and drain before use.
Rice (glutinous)	White colour. Use especially for making Chinese cakes and puddings.
Rice (long grain)	Use for everyday dishes with meat or vegetables.
Rice noodles	1 inch wide rice noodle also known as "Hor Fun" very popular in Penang, Malaysia. Use for stir-fry.
Rice noodles	A very fine noodle white known as "Mee -Sawar". Long life noodle.
Rice noodles	Another very fine transparent noodles known as "Tang- Hoon". Use for stir-fry or soup dishes.
Rice (purple)	Use for pudding only.
Rice Vermicellli	A fine white noodle sold in packets. Soak in water until soft before use. Known as "Bee Hoon" in Chinese.
Rice paper	Rice paper made from rice. Use for wrapping spring-rolls.

Rice vinegar	Use to flavour Sushi rice in Japan.
Rice wine	Japanese wine known as "Sake" in Japan.
Saffron	Looks like very fine orange thread. Use for colouring.
Seaweed	Dried black seaweed use for stir-fry dishes or use for wrapping Sushi rice. Also known as "Laver".
Sesame oil	Gives a nice flavour to meat dishes.
Sesame seeds	Gives a rich aroma when roasted, use to flavour meat dishes.
Shallots	Small red onions, which grow in groups. Use quite often in curry paste.
Star- anise	Flower shaped brown spice. Has aniseed flavour and aroma. Use very often in Malaya for cooking.
Star fruit	A star shaped yellow orange fruit with very sweet juicy flavour. Can be use for drinks.
Sugar cane	Long stems about 6 ft. tall. Use for making sugar and drinks.
Sushi rice	Special Japanese rice round shape, use for making Sushi rolls.
Sweet potatoes	Long shaped potato use for puddings.
Tamarind fruit	Sweet and sour fruit grows on trees. Made into a paste. Use for sweet and sour sauce and for curry dishes.
Turmeric powder	Ground yellow ginger use for flavouring curry dishes.
To-Fu	White firm, square creamy, beancurd known as "To-Fu".
Water chestnuts	Fresh and tin ones are available in Chinese supermarkets. Very crispy, can be use for salad or eat raw.
Yam	Brown coloured vegetable. Peel skin off before cooking. Can be use stir-fry or for puddings.

INDEX